DO YOU REMEMBER—

The 1940s . . . Who were the stars of CAPTAIN VIDEO AND HIS VIDEO RANGERS?

The 1950s . . . MR. PEEPERS' girlfriend and what she did for a living?

The 1960s . . . What made THE HATHAWAYS such an unusual family?

The 1970s . . . The names of the delightful ladies who portrayed THE SNOOP SISTERS?

HERE IS TELEVISION AT ITS BEST (AND WORST)—SOMETIMES WACKY, *ALWAYS* ENTERTAINING—A QUIZ BOOK TO TEST THE MOST HARDENED TV ADDICT!

Do You Remember?

Fred Goldstein

PINNACLE BOOKS   **NEW YORK**

DO YOU REMEMBER?

Copyright © 1982 by Fred Goldstein

An original Pinnacle Books edition, published for the first time anywhere.

First printing, May 1982

ISBN: 0-523-41629-6

Text layout and design by Michael Serrian

Printed in the United States of America

PINNACLE BOOKS, INC.
1430 Broadway
New York, New York 10018

DEDICATION

To Phyllis, my wife, whose love and devotion inspire and motivate me.

To Deb and Sher, my daughters, for their patience and understanding.

To Mom and Dad, who purchased the twelve-inch box that hooked me.

ACKNOWLEDGEMENT

A special thanks to my friend Ira Golden whose enthusiasm and cooperation was greatly appreciated.

Contents

Do You Remember?

Introduction

In 1951 my parents bought our first television set. I was immediately "hooked" and that's when I became a TV fan.

Most of us have grown up with the "tube" and the rest have spent a significant part of their lives with it. Television is one of the common denominators, like the weather and taxes, that transcends all walks of life; young and old, rich and poor, men and women.

You probably recall someone asking "Did you see the —— program last night" or the comments people make about programs: it was great, it was so-so, terrible, I forgot it was on, maybe I can see the rerun, etcetera.

Everybody has an opinion about television programs and everybody to some degree remembers shows, personalities, performers, characters, locations, and other bits and pieces about TV.

DO YOU REMEMBER provides the opportunity to look back at approximately a third of a century (1948–1978) of television and recall things you once knew and forgot, or find out what you never knew about many programs and performers.

Remembering is fun and sometimes profitable, particularly when you have a source like this available.

This book is divided into four sections. Each one represents a decade since commercial television's inception in the late 1940's. To help you recall or refer to the information presented, the questions, answers, and fall prime-time network program schedules are included on a yearly basis. Also featured is an album of selected program/performer photographs for each television season within the decade.

There are always limitations on the amount of information one can provide in this type of effort. If there are any specific questions that you would like answered about your favorite TV programs and/or if you would like to see more books like this one, please contact me in care of the publisher.

I sincerely hope you have many enjoyable hours traveling back through the years recalling TV memories. And when the question comes up *Do You Remember . . .* you will be able to provide the answer.

The 1940s

QUESTIONS

1948

1. What was one of television's earliest dramatic series, and what notable young actor made a very rare TV appearance during that first season on the air?
2. In addition to CBS, ABC, and NBC, what was the fourth television network that existed?
3. Long before he became Sergeant Bilko, Phil Silvers hosted one of television's early variety shows. What was the name of that show?
4. Tuesday nights was known as "Uncle Miltie night." What was the name of the program that was on opposite Milton Berle for two years?
5. NBC's Friday night boxing telecasts were known by the program title _____ _____ _____. Who provided the commentary?
6. Bob Smith, better known for his association with Howdy Doody, hosted this half-hour NBC variety show. Name it.
7. One of the first shows on the ABC network offered young performers the chance to enhance their careers by appearing in dramatic roles with estab-

lished stars. What was the name of the program, and who was the host during most of its run?

8. The second longest-running network TV program began in 1948 and ran until 1979. Name that show.

9. Dennis James hosted one of TV's first daytime shows on the Dumont network. What was it?

10. One of the first magazine-type shows on television was on the NBC network in 1948. It was co-hosted by a gentleman who went on to become a famous television newscaster, and a lady who eventually became a member of Congress. Name the show, and the co-hosts.

11. ARTHUR GODFREY'S TALENT SCOUTS was one of the most popular programs in the early days of television. How long was it on?

12. A very popular radio show commenced on television in the summer of 1948. It was the first regular series to be simulcast on both network radio and network television. Name the program and its original host.

13. One of TV's first popular female personalities was at one time a Hollywood starlet who achieved much success in the early days of this new medium. Who was she?

14. A young and promising crooner of the day was only twenty-one years old when he began his first television show in 1948. Who was he?

15. What was the name of TV's first regularly scheduled mystery series and which network was it on?

16. We are all familiar with Julia Child as TV's most popular contemporary cook. In the early days of television _____ _____ was held in the same esteem. She hosted a show entitled TO THE QUEEN'S TASTE.

17. Joe Howard, a show biz trooper dating back to the 1890s, and who also wrote the song HELLO MY BABY, emceed this old-fashioned variety show first on radio and then television. Name that TV show.

18. A major radio star of the '40s was one of the first entertainers to venture into television on a regular

basis. What was his name and what was his first network show?

19. What cello-stroking comic hosted a comedy/variety series in a nightclub setting which began on CBS? Name the comic and the club.

20. On what night of the week was the PABST BLUE RIBBON BOUTS seen and who was the first ringside announcer?

21. One of network television's earliest domestic situation comedy shows starred a real-life husband and wife team. Name the show and its stars.

22. As unlikely as it may seem, one of TV's earliest personalities was an artist. His program, one of the first instructional shows, actually began in 1946. Who was this artist, and what was the name of his show?

23. One of television's first game shows was hosted by Bill Slater. Name the show.

24. One of radio's all-time favorite female personalities hosted a talk show for many years. For a short time in 1948 she did the same on television. Who was she?

1949

1. A Friday night TV variety hour, which was broadcast on two networks simultaneously, provided the first regular starring role for one of television's outstanding comedians. Name the show and the comedian.
2. THE ALDRICH FAMILY was one of the first successful television situation comedy programs. Name the town and street where the Aldrich family lived.
3. What was the name of the first TV game show to be hosted by a woman, and who was she?
4. One of television's all-time favorite space shows was CAPTAIN VIDEO AND HIS VIDEO RANGERS. There were two actors who starred in this role. Can you name them?
5. Name the variety show on the Dumont television network which was a springboard for many of Jackie Gleason's characters.
6. THE KAY KYSER KOLLEGE OF MUSICAL KNOWLEDGE was a popular musical quiz show. Featured on this program was a vocalist who went on to talk-show fame. Name that vocalist.
7. One of the first game shows developed by Mark Goodson and Bill Todman began on radio in 1946 and commenced on television in 1948 with Bud Collyer as the host. Name the show.

8. One of television's most durable prime-time game shows had a format which consisted of two teams of celebrities playing charades. Name the show and the host.

9. A very popular quiz show, which commenced on radio in the mid-forties, began its television run on the ABC network, and ultimately ran on each of the networks during its long tenure. Name the show and the host most often remembered.

10. One of the first documentary series filmed especially for TV was a series of twenty-six half-hour episodes based on General Dwight D. Eisenhower's book about the American effort in Europe during World War II. Name the program and narrator.

11. Walter Burns was the editor of a small-town newspaper in this short-run series which was based on a film of the same title. What was the name of the series and who played Walter Burns.

12. A prime-time musical variety show broadcast from Chicago was hosted by this personality who was being introduced to the national television audience. In later years he went on to greater national fame as the host of a show that still exists. Name the personality and the musical variety show he hosted.

13. THE GOLDBERGS, starring Molly Goldberg, had long been a favorite on radio and then became one of TV's most popular situation comedies. The setting of the show was in the Bronx, New York. What was the address of the apartment house where they lived?

14. Who played Hopalong Cassidy's sidekick and what was his name?

15. One of the early talk shows featured a regular panel of female celebrities giving the women's view on a variety of subjects. What was the name of the program and who was the hostess?

16. Another favorite radio situation comedy to make the transition to television was THE LIFE OF RILEY. Who first played Chester Riley and Peg Riley when the series began on television?

17. One of TV's first popular family situation comedies

9

was MAMA. This was a story about a Norwegian family living in San Francisco. Name the characters and who played them.

18. Mike Barnett was the principal character in a program about a New York City private detective who did not use a gun. Name the program and the actor who portrayed Barnett.

19. Another tough private eye from New York also made his debut on television about the same time as Mike Barnett. His name was Martin Kane. Who originally played this character?

20. One of the more appealing shows on the Dumont network was a thirty-minute police drama in which the lead role or star was never seen. To achieve this technique the camera was employed as the actor, and therefore viewers saw everything as the character did. What was the name of the show and who was the unseen star?

21. The first of the big television circus programs began during 1949 and was broadcast from Chicago. Name the show, the ringmaster, and his assistant.

22. The Libby Company sponsored an unusual program which was broadcast from Chicago. Both the studio audience and the home viewer were able to participate simultaneously while the program was being telecast. Name the program and explain how it worked.

23. This thirty-minute prime-time game show featured female contestants who competed in various game quizzes and stunts for valuable prizes. Originally this was a long-running and popular radio show. Name the program and the hosts.

24. A popular thriller and suspense drama began each week with only a close shot of a pair of eyes, then a bloody hand reaching to turn out the lights, followed by an eerie laugh. What was the name of this program and who was the first host?

Photo Album

Question 1:
This happy group spent many years together on television. From left to right, what are their full names?

Question 2:
Like many other housewives this lady loved to talk and gossip with her neighbor. How did she get her neighbor's attention?

Question 3:
This man cannot believe what his wife just told him. Who are the characters portrayed?

13

Prime-Time Network Program Schedules

		7PM		7:30		8PM		8:30
Sunday	ABC			Southern-Aires Quartet	Pauline Fredericks	Hollywood Screen Test		Actors Studio
	CBS	Newsweek in Review		Studio One				Riddle Me This
	NBC	Mary Kaye and Johnny	News	Welcome Aboard		Author Meets The Critic		Meet the Press
Monday	ABC	News		Kiernan's Corner		Quizzing the News		Film
	CBS		Places Please	News	Face The Music			Arthur Godfrey's Talent Scouts
	NBC				News	Tele-Theatre		Americana
Tuesday	ABC	News						America's
	CBS	Roar of The Rails		News	Face the Music			
	NBC				News		The Texaco Star Theater (The Milton Berle Show)	
Wednesday	ABC	News		Critic at large		Gay Nineties Revue		Three About Town
	CBS		Places Please	News	Face The Music			Winner Take All
	NBC	Birthday Party	You Are An Artist	News	Girl About Town			
Thursday	ABC	News				Fashion Story		Club Seven
	CBS			News	Face The Music	Dione Lucas Cooking Show		Movie
	NBC		Paris Cavalcade of Fashion	Musical Miniatures	News	NBCs Presents	Nature of Things	The Swift Show
Friday	ABC	News		Red Caboose	Film Shorts	Candid Microphone		Various
	CBS		Places Please	News	Face The Music	What Is It Worth		Capt. Billy's Music Hall
	NBC			Musical Merry Go Round	News	Musical Miniatures		Stop Me If You've Heard This One
Saturday	ABC	News		Sports		Play The Game		
	CBS							
	NBC		Television Screen Magazine	Saturday Night Jamboree				

Question 1:
STUDIO ONE was initially sponsored by what appliance manufacturer?

NETWORK SCHEDULE

9PM	9:30	10PM	10:30	11PM		
	Movie				ABC	Sunday
	Toast of the Town		America Speaks	News	CBS	Sunday
	Philco Television Playhouse				NBC	Sunday
	Film				ABC	Monday
	Sporting Event				CBS	Monday
News Reel	Boxing				NBC	Monday
	Town Meeting				ABC	Tuesday
We The People	People's Platform				CBS	Tuesday
Mary Margaret McBride		Wrestling			NBC	Tuesday
		Wrestling			ABC	Wednesday
		Boxing			CBS	Wednesday
	Kraft Television Theater	News Reel	The Village Barn		NBC	Wednesday
		Movie			ABC	Thursday
	Sports				CBS	Thursday
Gulf Road Show	Bigelow Show				NBC	Thursday
Break the Bank					ABC	Friday
					CBS	Friday
I'd Like To See	News	Gillette Cavalcade of Sports			NBC	Friday
					ABC	Saturday
					CBS	Saturday
					NBC	Saturday

17

		7PM	7:30	8PM	8:30
Sunday	ABC	Paul Whiteman Revue	Penthouse Payers	Think Fast	Little Revue
	CBS	Tonight on Broadway	This Is Show Business	Toast of The Town	
	NBC	Leave It To The Girls	Aldrich Family	Chesterfield Supper Club	Colgate Theatre
Monday	ABC				
	CBS	Roar of The Rails	News	Sonny Kendis	Silver Theater	Arthur Godfrey's Talent Scouts
	NBC	Kukla, Fran and Ollie	Mohawk Showroom	News	Tele-Theater	Voice of Firestone
Tuesday	ABC				
	CBS	Strictly for Laughs	News	Sonny Kendis	Movies/Specials	
	NBC	Kukla, Fran and Ollie	Mohawk Show Room	News	The Texaco Star Theater (The Milton Berle Show)	
Wednesday	ABC			Photoplay Time	Photocrime
	CBS	Strictly For Laughs	News	At Home	Arthur Godfrey & His Friends	
	NBC	Kukla, Fran and Ollie	Mohawk Showroom	News	Crisis	The Clock
Thursday	ABC			Stop the Music	
	CBS	Dione Lucas	News	Sonny Kendis	The Front Page	Inside U.S.A./ Romance
	NBC	Kukla, Fran and Ollie	Mohawk Showroom	News	Hollywood Premiere	Mary Kay and Johnny
Friday	ABC			Majority Rules	Blind Date
	CBS	Strictly For Laughs	News	Sonny Kendis	Mama	Man Against Crime
	NBC	Kukla Fran and Ollie	Mohawk Showroom	News	One Man's Family	We the People
Saturday	ABC		Hollywood Screen Test	Paul Whiteman's TV Teen Club	
	CBS			Blues By Bargy	
	NBC			Nature of Things	News

Question 2:
Who hosted the variety program THIS IS SHOW BUSINESS?

NETWORK SCHEDULE

9PM	9:30	10PM	10:30	11PM		
Let There Be Stars		Celebrity Time	Youth on the March		ABC	Sunday
Fred Waring Show		News			CBS	Sunday
Philco Television Playhouse		Garroway at Large			NBC	Sunday
Mr. Black					ABC	Monday
Candid Camera	The Goldbergs	Studio One			CBS	Monday
Lights Out	Band of America	Quiz Kids			NBC	Monday
	On Trial		Boxing		ABC	Tuesday
Actors Studio	Suspense	This Week in Sports	Blues By Bargy	Pantomine Quiz	CBS	Tuesday
Fireside Theater	Life of Riley	Ted Mack's Amateur Hour			NBC	Tuesday
		Wrestling			ABC	Wednesday
Bigelow Show		Boxing (Pabst Blue Ribbon Bouts)			CBS	Wednesday
Kraft Television Theater		Break the Bank			NBC	Wednesday
Crusade in Europe	Starring Boris Karloff	Roller Derby			ABC	Thursday
Ed Wynn Show					CBS	Thursday
Fireball Fun-For All		Martin Kane			NBC	Thursday
Auction-Aire	Fun or The Money	Roller Derby			ABC	Friday
Ford Theater/ 54th Street Revue		People's Platform	Capitol Clochroom		CBS	Friday
Versatile Varieties	Big Stokey	Gillette Cavalcade of Sports			NBC	Friday
	Roller Derby				ABC	Saturday
					CBS	Saturday
Who Said That	Meet The Press				NBC	Saturday

19

ANSWERS

1948

1. ACTORS STUDIO — Marlon Brando
2. DUMONT
3. THE ARROW SHOW
4. COURT OF CURRENT ISSUES
5. GILLETTE CAVALCADE OF SPORTS — Jimmy Powers
6. THE GULF ROAD SHOW
7. HOLLYWOOD SCREEN TEST — Neil Hamilton
8. LAMP UNTO MY FEET
9. OKAY MOTHER
10. TV SCREEN MAGAZINE — John K. McCaffery, Millicent Fenwick
11. Ten years
12. WE, THE PEOPLE — Dwight Weist
13. Wendy Barrie
14. Alan Dale
15. BARNEY BLAKE, POLICE REPORTER — NBC
16. Dione Lucas
17. THE GAY NINETIES REVUE

18. Henry Morgan — ON THE CORNER
19. Morey Amsterdam — GOLDEN GOOSE CAFE
20. Wednesday — Russ Hodges
21. MARY KAY AND JOHNNY — Mary Kay and Johnny Stearns
22. Jon Gnagy — YOU ARE AN ARTIST
23. CHARADE QUIZ
24. Mary Margaret McBride

1949

1. ADMIRAL BROADWAY REVUE — Sid Caesar
2. Centerville, Elm Street
3. BLIND DATE — Arlene Francis
4. Richard Coogan, Al Hodge
5. CAVALCADE OF STARS
6. Mike Douglas
7. WINNER TAKE ALL
8. PANTOMIME QUIZ — Mike Stokey
9. BREAK THE BANK — Bert Parks
10. CRUSADE IN EUROPE — Westbrook Van Voorhis
11. THE FRONT PAGE — John Daly
12. Dave Garroway — GARROWAY AT LARGE
13. 1030 East Tremont Avenue
14. Edgar Buchanan — Red Connors
15. LEAVE IT TO THE GIRLS — Maggi McNallis
16. Jackie Gleason and Rosemary DeCamp
17. Mama (Marta Hansen) . Peggy Wood
    Poppa (Lars Hansen) .. Judson Laire
    Katrin .... Rosemary Rice
    Nels .... Dick Van Patten
    Robin .... originally Iris Mann, then
                          Robin Morgan

18. MEN AGAINST CRIME — Ralph Bellamy
19. William Gargan
20. THE PLAINCLOTHESMAN — Ken Lynch
21. SUPER CIRCUS — Claude Kirchner and Mary Hartline
22. AUCTION-AIRE — The video audience and home-viewers bid for valuable prizes, using not cash, but labels from the sponsor, Libby Foods Products.
23. LADIES BE SEATED — Tom Moore, Phil Patton
24. LIGHTS OUT — Jack LaRue

THE 1940s PHOTO AND PROGRAM SCHEDULE ANSWERS

Photo answers

1. Kukla, Burr Tillstrom, Oliver J. Dragon, and Fran Allison
2. By opening the window and calling "Yoo-hoo, Mrs. Bloom."
3. Chester A. and Peg Riley

Program Schedule Answers

1. Westinghouse
2. Clifton Fadiman

The 1950s

QUESTIONS

1950

1. BEULAH was the story about a maid with a heart of gold, and the first situation comedy to star a black performer. Who played Beulah?

2. BIG TOP was the CBS network's first big circus show. Originating from Convention Hall in Camden, New Jersey, it featured a well known radio personality as the ringmaster. Also a very well known television personality of today made his first national appearance as one of the resident clowns on this show. Name the ringmaster and the clown.

3. Lorelei Kilbourne was the society columnist on this illustrated press, a crusading daily newspaper, and the close associate of the paper's chief crime-fighting reporter. Name this popular TV show, and who originally played the crime-fighting reporter and society columnist.

4. BROADWAY OPEN HOUSE was network television's first regularly scheduled late night program. Jerry Lester is usually the host most people associate

with the show. However Lester was only on three nights of the week. Who was the host on the other two nights of the week?

5. On BROADWAY OPEN HOUSE a young actress, Jennie Lewis, played the role of a dumb blonde named Dagmar. What was Jennie Lewis' real name?

6. BUCK ROGERS in the twenty-fifth century originally appeared on television in 1950. Who played Buck Rogers?

7. The popular radio comedy team of George Burns and Gracie Allen brought to television a situation comedy series in which they played themselves. Their next-door neighbors were Harry and Blanche Morton. Who originally played these characters?

8 THE ED SULLIVAN SHOW, on Sunday nights, was a television fixture. However, NBC introduced a program that competed successfully with Ed Sullivan during the first four years it was on the air. Name that show.

9. What musical variety show used a campus soda shop as its background setting and starred a member of a famous comedy team?

10. This comedy/mystery program was a summer replacement for MAN AGAINST CRIME, a popular detective series. Lynn Barri and Donald Curtis were the stars of the show. What was the name of the program?

11. CBS's first television soap opera began in 1950 and did not turn out too well, lasting less than two years. What was the name of this early TV soap?

12. Another half-hour crime show featuring a crusading newspaper columnist made its debut this year. What was the name of the program and the star?

13. This live hour-long dramatic series was seen on Tuesday night opposite Milton Berle's TEXACO STAR THEATER. It featured such outstanding stars as Helen Hayes, Bert Lahr, Grace Kelly, Walter Abel, and many more. What was the name of this program?

14. Captain John Braddock was the principal character

in this very popular police drama. Name the program and the star.

15. Gala Poochie, Polka Dottie, El Squeako, and Poison Zoomack were all characters on this popular children's show. Name the program and its host.

16. This hour-long musical program was a showcase for aspiring amateur songwriters, whose songs were performed by such guest vocalists as Rosemary Clooney, Tony Bennett, Toni Arden, and Richard Hays. Name the show and its first host.

17. SPACE PATROL was another popular space program of the day. The central character was Buzz Corey. The Commander-in-Chief of the space patrol, who was always battling space villains using his ship which he called the greatest in the universe. Who played Commander Corey, and what was the name of his ship?

18. THE STU ERWIN SHOW was one of early typical situation comedy type shows about a bumbling father, his level-headed wife, and two teenage children. What was Dad's occupation?

19. What major motion picture star of today appeared in a comedy series about a pompous theater critic and his man servant?

20. CAPTAIN VIDEO, SPACE PATROL, and a third popular space show were all on television in 1950. Name that show and who played the principal character.

21. What action drama show based on the files of the United States Treasury Department began its five year network run on ABC, and who was the star of the show?

22. WHAT'S MY LINE was television's longest-running prime-time game show. During that time there was only one host, John Daly. Who were the panelists on the first show?

23. YOUR SHOW OF SHOWS was one of television's most ambitious undertakings. Each week there were ninety minutes of live entertainment. Sid Caeser's

comedy genius developed many characters. Amongst them were The Jazz Musician, The Story Teller, and The Italian Film Authority. Can you name them?

24. An interesting program which answered viewer requests for just about anything, enjoyed a long tenure on television. Name the show and the original host.

1951

1. A summer replacement for the popular MAMA show featured Peter Donald as the host and a young husband and wife acting team. The husband went on to become an outstanding actor, winning two Oscars. Name the actor and the show.
2. Current 60 MINUTES news correspondent Mike Wallace hosted a half-hour interview show with his wife, at the time (1951), about the goings on of New York City. Name the show and the co-hostess.
3. A one-time master criminal turned private detective, who already was popular because Chester Morris had portrayed him in several motion pictures, was the main character in this half-hour series. Name the character and who played him.
4. A 1947 movie starring Claudette Colbert became television's first comedy serial. This fifteen minute series ran five days a week, and was about the owners of a run-down chicken farm. What was the name of the serial and who were the stars?
5. IT'S NEWS TO ME was the name of a prime-time game show where contestants were involved with current events. Interestingly enough, this show was hosted by various newsmen of the day. Name at least two of the hosts.

6. An exciting wartime adventure series seen on the Dumont network revolved around the activities of an American agent in China during World War II. Eric Fleming, the star of many "B" movies, played this lead role. Name the character and the show.

7. MR. DISTRICT ATTORNEY was a very popular radio police drama whose popularity continued on television. What was the district attorney's name and who first played the role on television?

8. An unusual western adventure series presented its star in a different character role each week. This star was at one time a world championship rodeo rider. Name the program and its star.

9. A popular western adventure about the pilot/owner of the Flying Crown Ranch in Arizona was titled SKY KING. Who played Sky King and what was the name of his plane?

10. A quiz show in which contestants revealed to the home viewers and studio audience their most pressing problems was known as "The Show With A Heart." What was the name of the show and who was the emcee?

11. Pinky Lee was one of the stars of a fifteen-minute musical comedy/variety series that was on three nights a week. Who originally was the other star and what was the name of the show?

12. New York City was the background for this sitcom about two sisters trying to become fashion models. The characters' names were Babs and Peggy Smith. Coincidentally the two actresses who played these characters were named Peggy. What were their surnames, and what was the title of this show?

13. One of the more durable prime-time shows on the Dumont network was a quiz program depicting famous events which were dramatized on stage. A panel of well known newspaper columnists were invited each week to identify these events. Name the show and any of the four hosts.

14. A famous U.S. Marshal of the old west was Wild Bill Hickok. He and his sidekick Jingles fought many

battles against injustice. What were Hickok and Jingles' full names?

15. The two longest-running daytime serials began on CBS in 1951. Name them.

16. SCHLITZ PLAYHOUSE OF STARS was a long running dramatic anthology series which began on October 5, 1951. What famous Broadway star was in the premiere telecast?

17. AMOS AND ANDY, the long-running and popular radio series, began its initial run on television in the summer of 1951. Who played the following characters:
    A) Amos B) Andy C) George "The Kingfish" Stevens D) Sapphire Stevens

18. Oogie Pringle was the boyfriend of _____ _____ in the situation comedy ___ ____ _____ ____ on ABC.

19. One of television's most intelligent panel shows, DOWN YOU GO, achieved the distinction of being on all four networks during its life span. Who was the host throughout most of its run?

20. Casey was a press photographer for the Morning Express in the crime drama program _____ _____, originally starring _____ _____.

21. MEET CORLISS ARCHER, one of America's most popular teenagers on radio, became a live TV weekly series. Who played Corliss Archer?

22. Throughout its many years on television who portrayed Mr. WIZARD in the educational series of the same name?

23. THE RANGE RIDER and his sidekick Dick West roamed the West defending justice in a popular weekly thirty-minute western series. Who played THE RANGE RIDER and the sidekick?

24. Can you name one or two of the earliest adult science fiction programs?

1952

1. HALLMARK HALL OF FAME, which is still on television today, originally started as a thirty-minute show and was titled HALLMARK TELEVISION PLAYHOUSE. At that time the show had a hostess who occasionally starred in some of the productions. Who was she?

2. A husband and wife American spy team posing as export/import buyers, were the two principal characters in this adventure series. Name the show and its stars.

3. A situation comedy in which the head of a construction company was a woman was titled _____ _____ and starred _____ _____ .

4. Dr. Barton Crane was the principal character in one of TV's earliest medical shows. Who played this role and what was the name of the program?

5. A late-night show featuring a suave, debonair batchelor who wooed the ladies in a very romantic setting was a fifteen-minute program aired two nights of the week. Name the show and the star.

6. Long before THE WILD WILD WEST there were United States government undercover agents in the old West. Pat Gallagher and Stoney Crockett were

the agents. What was the name of the program and who were the stars?

7. Steve Mitchell was the government agent in this adventure series which was originally a popular radio program. Name this show and the star.

8. A western anthology series began its long run on television in 1952. The first host was known as the Old Ranger. What was the name of the program and who was the Old Ranger?

9. This fifteen-minute domestic comedy was seen on Tuesday and Thursday and was about the trials and tribulations of newlyweds. The characters' names were Pete and Betsy Bell; incidentally, in real life they were also married. Name the show and the stars.

10. THE HUNTER was an international intrigue series which was concerned with the adventures of an American undercover agent fighting Communism in the western world. What was The Hunter's name and who originally played him?

11. MEET MILLIE was a popular sitcom about a young secretary living with a mother who was eager for her to find a husband. Who played the role of Millie and what actress portrayed her mother?

12. MR. PEEPERS was popular situation comedy and starred Wally Cox in the title role. What was Mr. Peepers' occupation and where did he work?

13. _____ _____ was Mr. Peepers' girlfriend. What was her occupation and who played her?

14. The principal character in this comedy series was described as a beautiful, wacky, and not-too-bright secretary. She and her roommate lived in Mrs. O'Reilly's rooming house on Manhattan's West Side. What was the name of the program, character, star, and who played her roommate?

15. Robert Beanblossom was a real estate salesman working for the _____ _____ Company in the comedy series _____ _____ starring _____ _____.

16. A comedian who had had considerable experience in

burlesque came to television in a comedy/variety show which was a smash hit, particularly in its first season. He opened the show with his theme song, "The Ho-Ho Song." Who is this comic and what was the first line of his theme song?

17. A short-run international intrigue adventure series used as its background setting a posh nightclub in Paris, France. Ilona Massey was the female star. Name the program and the male star.

18. What was the name of the quiz show which was Jack Parr's first network television series?

19. VICTORY AT SEA was one of television's outstanding documentary series which began its initial run in 1952. Who composed the musical score, and who narrated the series?

20. THE ADVENTURES OF OZZIE AND HARRIET was network television's longest running situation comedy.
A) What was the name of their next-door neighbor, and who played him?
B) What was the Nelsons' address?

21. TODAY was network television's first early morning program, and Dave Garroway was the initial host. What two individuals assisted Garroway with the sports, news, and other features on this show?

22. LIFE WITH LUIGI was another example of a popular radio program which had far less success on television. J. Carrol Naish originally played Luigi Bosco. Who played Luigi after Mr. Naish left the show?

23. OUR MISS BROOKS was a very popular comedy about a high school English teacher, Connie Brooks, played by Eve Arden. One of her students spoke in a high-pitched voice. What was his name, and who played him?

24. A police anthology series that featured in various episodes such stars as E.G. Marshall, Edward Binns, and James Gregory, was a thirty-minute show that had the same name as one that was popular during the 1970s. What was the name of this show?

1953

1. Ezio Pinza was the star of an ethnic situation comedy about a widowed Italian American opera singer who had a large family. His oldest son Edward was played by an actor who in the late seventies played a father in one of the top network comedies. Name the program Ezio Pinza starred in and who played his son.
2. Rod Cameron played the starring role of a tough New York cop in this half-hour series. Name the program and the character he played.
3. Alan Mowbray, one of Hollywood's best known character actors, was the star of this situation comedy about a con man's con man. What was the name of this show?
4. A popular dramatic series about an American counter-spy starred Richard Carlson as the principal character. Name the program and the real-life person Richard Carlson portrayed.
5. Brandon DeWilde was the child star of this ABC situation comedy about a youngster whose parents had been killed, and who lived with his relatives. Name the show and the character Branden DeWilde played.
6. On this thirty-minute crime show the story revolved around a young Korean war veteran who joined the

New York City police force. William Redfield starred as this principal character. Name the show.

7. This was the year a dramatic anthology series commenced on Tuesday nights at ten o'clock on the NBC television network, and was to run eight years in this time slot. What was the name of this show?

8. MAKE ROOM FOR DADDY was one of the more popular situation comedies as evidenced by its long tenure, over ten years. Name the original family members and who played them.

9. An interesting crime series that was based on true stories of men and women from the files of various law enforcement agencies, such as Offices of The Public-Defender, Correction Department Parole Office, Forestry Department, U.S. Army Military Police, and more, was titled ____ ____ _____ ____ _____ starring _____ _____.

10. MY FAVORITE HUSBAND was a domestic comedy about a successful banker and his beautiful but scatterbrained wife. Barry Nelson played the husband, George Cooper. What two actresses played Liz Cooper, his wife?

11. Jeffrey Lynn was Dr. Robert Allison, Anne Sargent was Barbara Miller the doctor's receptionist, and Martin Huston was the doctor's son. What was the name of this program?

12. Edward R. Murrow's PERSON TO PERSON program gave viewers an opportunity to see celebrities being interviewed in the comfort of their homes. What celebrities appeared on the first show?

13. Susie MacNamara, a private secretary, in this show of the same name, was played by Ann Sothern. What was the name of her boss, and who played him?

14. This Academy Award-winning actor was the central character in an early space adventure series which was popular with Saturday morning viewers. It was the only continuing series this actor ever starred in on television. Name the actor and the program.

15. A daytime serial about a young woman, Poco Thurman, who leaves a small town and comes to New

York City to become a model, ran for approximately one and one-half years on the NBC network. What was the name of this soap opera?

16. Strange as it may seem, there was a live western broadcast on weekday afternoons. The setting of this series was in Montana and starred Jack Valentine, and featured Mary Elaine Watt, and Barry Cassell. What was the name of this western?

17. The Modernaires were a featured musical group on what musical variety show?

18. George Jessel was the first host of this heartwarming series which resembled THIS IS YOUR LIFE. The series highlighted people, particularly celebrities, who fought to rebuild their lives. What was the name of this program?

19. A situation comedy that was a regular fifteen-minute segment of THE KATE SMITH HOUR was given its own half-hour on Saturday nights at seven-thirty. The setting was in the town of Sandy Harbor and the plot was about the trials and tribulations of a happily married middle-aged couple. Name the program, and who played the principal characters.

20. LIFE WITH FATHER was a successful Hollywood movie and Broadway play before it became a television series. Who played the father and the mother in this program?

21. A very famous Hollywood film actor who usually played a gangster was a cop in this police drama. Name the star and the program.

22. What was the name of a public affairs program that was hosted by a former U. S. Vice President, and who was he?

23. One of television's outstanding dramatic programs, THE U.S. STEEL HOUR, began in 1953. How many years did it run?

24. An unusual program which recreated famous events, employed actual correspondents to interview the principal figures involved was titled ＿＿ ＿＿ ＿＿＿ and was narrated by ＿＿＿ ＿＿＿＿＿.

1954

1. CAPTAIN MIDNIGHT was a very popular radio adventure series that began on television in 1954. Midnight had an assistant who was a mechanic, and known to everyone as Icky. Who played Captain Midnight? What was Icky's full name, and name the actor who played him.
2. In this situation comedy a college professor gives up teaching to become an advisor-to-the-lovelorn columnist on a large city newspaper. What was the name of this program, the character, and who starred in the role?
3. A fun game show in which celebrity panelists were asked to think of captions for line drawings was entitled DROODLES. Carl Reiner was among the regular panelists each week. Who was the host?
4. Ed Gardner, created the role of Archie, the manager of DUFFY'S TAVERN from the show of the same name. What was the famous saying Archie used at the opening of the show?
5. Paul Gilbert, Allen Jenkins, and Phyllis Coates were the stars of this situation comedy about a professional prizefighter who quits the ring to open a nightclub. What was the name of this program?
6. On this quiz show, members of the studio audience

were asked where they would like to go on vacation and why. The people with the best responses were selected to be contestants and received the opportunity to win an all-expenses paid vacation to the place of their choice. Name the quiz show and the host.

7. FATHER KNOWS BEST, the story of the Anderson family, was one of television's outstanding family comedies. Including reruns, the program was on all three networks and in one particular year it was number six in the ratings amongst all programs. Name the family members and who played them.

8. Jack Klugman and Martin Balsam had minor roles in this short-lived daytime serial about the trials and tribulations of a woman physician. What was the name of this soap opera?

9. Celeste Holm starred in this comedy series about a journalism teacher from a midwestern college who takes a job on a New York City newspaper. Name the character she played and the title of the show.

10. THE INNER SANCTUM, a dramatic series of scary tales, was a long-time popular radio program that had far less success on television. Most of us are aware of the show's trademark, a squeaking door, but what was the name of the unseen host who invited the audience each week "to the inner sanctum," and who played him?

11. IT'S A GREAT LIFE was a comedy about two ex-GIs who decided to move to southern California to seek civilian employment. Episodes centered around their problems getting new jobs and the trouble they got themselves into with money-making schemes. What were the names of these two characters and who played them?

12. Television's first series about a nurse was titled _____ _____ _____ _____ and starred _____ _____.

13. JOE PALOOKA, the lovable naïve pugilist, came to life for a short period of time on television in 1954. Who played him?

14. The National Legal Aid Society and The Legal Aid Society of New York provided the material for the stories presented on this particular half-hour drama. Dane Clark played one of the lead roles. Who played the other, and what was the name of the program?

15. San Francisco was background for this police drama. Lieutenant Ben Guthrie and Inspector Matt Grebb were the principal characters. Name the actors who played them and the title of the program.

16. Believe it or not the United States Postal Service was the background and provided the material for the stories presented in this series. Name either the original title or second title by which this series was known.

17. THE MARRIAGE was a comedy series that lasted only eight episodes. Even though its life span was so short it had the distinction of being one of the first prime-time programs to be telecast in color. What was the name of the family in the show and what husband and wife in real life played the same roles in this show?

18. Comedienne Martha Raye starred in her own comedy/variety show for several years beginning in 1954. Martha had a "pal" who was featured in most of her shows. At one time he was a famous professional boxer. Who was he?

19. Jim Davis, more recently known to the world as Jock Ewing, J.R.'s father, was the star of a western series about a detective who worked for the Southwestern Railroad. Name the program.

20. "Jarring" Jack Jackson, a former college football star, tried continuously to get his son junior interested in athletics. The lad had neither the inclination or ability to excel in sports. Neverthless the father was always trying. This series was based upon a movie of the same title. What was the name of the show and who played the father?

21. Preston Foster played a tugboat captain in this adventure series set in the San Pedro California

harbor. Name the program, principal character, and tugboat.

22. In Willy, Willa Dodger was a female attorney and the lead character in this series which took place in a small New England town. The actress who played the role was already well known to theater and motion picture audiences. Who was she?

23. Steve Allen was the first host of the TONIGHT SHOW. Who was his announcer/sidekick?

24. The CBS television network's counterpart to NBC's MEET THE PRESS began in 1954. Name the program and the two moderators who have been associated with the program over these many years.

1955

1. Midnight The Cat, Squeekie The Mouse, and Froggy The Gremlin were characters on this popular children's program. The show had been on television for several years running in prime-time, and then on Saturday mornings. Upon the death of the original host a second took over, and the show continued for five more years. Name the original host and program name, and the second host, and the revised title.
2. Keena Nomkeena, a real American Indian, was one of the cast members in this western series which dramatized stories from the Indians' point of view. What was the name of the program, and who was the star?
3. Captain Michael Gallant and Cuffy Sanders were two characters in an adventure that took place in North Africa. Depending upon when or where it was showing, the program was known under two titles. Name either of the titles and who played the above characters.
4. Television's longest-running network children's program began in 1955. Name the show and its star.
5. WARNER BROTHERS PRESENTS was the overall title for four rotating programs in this series. One of

them was based on a classic movie in a North African setting. Name the program and the male star.

6. Who played the role of Edward Dantes, the Count Of Monte Cristo in the syndicated television series.

7. Forrest Tucker and Sandy Kenyon were the stars in the adventure series about the owners of a charter boat service. Name the show and the characters they played.

8. Freelance writer Matt Anders was the principal character in this international intrigue series. Name the show and star.

9. FURY was the story of an orphan boy and his horse living on a ranch in the custody of the owner, a policeman. Peter Graves played Jim Newton, the adult lead. Who played the orphan boy?

10. Throckmorton P. Gildersleeve was the pompous water commissioner in the comedy series THE GREAT GILDERSLEEVE. What was the name of the town he lived in and who starred as Gildersleeve?

11. IT'S ALWAYS JAN was a situation comedy about a nightclub singer who was a single parent bringing up her child, while trying to further her career. Who was the star of this show?

12. Joe Sparton and Mabel Stooler were the principal characters in this comedy series about a cab driver and his girlfriend, a manicurist, who desires to become his wife. What was the name of the show and who played the characters?

13. Suave and sophisticated Bob Collins, photographer, played by Robert Cummings in THE BOB CUMMINGS SHOW (LOVE THAT BOB) was a bachelor who lived with his widowed sister and her son. Who played the widowed sister and her teenage son?

14. THE MIGHTY MOUSE PLAYHOUSE was a long-running Saturday morning carton show. Who was the voice of Mighty Mouse?

15. Pearl River, New York was the setting for this situation comedy about the vice president of a bank and his family. It was one of the early shows to be

filmed in color and appropriately sponsored by Eastman Kodak. Name the show and the star.

16. Dr. Tom Wilson was a child psychologist who was able to solve all child/family-related problems. However, in this situation comedy he had trouble raising his own children. Name the show and star.

17. THE ADVENTURES OF ROBIN HOOD became a Monday night fixture on CBS running for three consecutive years in the seven-thirty to eight o'clock time slot. All of the episodes were filmed on location in England which added to the show's credibility. Name the actor who starred as the legendary hero.

18. SCIENCE FICTION THEATRE presented stories about man's ability to reveal the mysteries of science and nature. What was the name of the bass-voiced host of the show?

19. A series about an American espionage agent involved in situations that threatened United States security was titled _____ _____ _____ and starred _____ _____.

20. SERGEANT PRESTON OF THE YUKON was a popular radio series which achieved a fair amount of success in television. Preston was always accompanied on all his adventures by his faithful dog and horse. Name the actor who played Preston and what were the names of his dog and horse?

21. Queenie Dugan and Kim Tracey were the principal characters in a situation comedy about trying to make it in show business. What was the name of the show, and who were the stars?

22. Phil Silvers as Sergeant Bilko was one of television's all-time favorite characters. Fill in the following:
    A) What was Bilko's full rank? _____
    B) What company and division was he in? _____
    C) What was the name of the camp?_____
    D) Which was part of what Fort? _____
    E) Located near what city? _____

23. THE LIFE AND LEGEND OF WYATT EARP was one of the better adult westerns that appeared on

television in the fifties. During its six-year original network run the program was amongst the top twenty rated shows in three of the years. What day, time, and network was it on, and over the years what were the names of the two towns were Earp was marshal?

24. GUNSMOKE became the longest running western on prime-time television lasing twenty years. What characters were with the program throughout its run?

1956

1. What all-time movie great made one of his rare appearances on television in a story entitled "Soldier From The Wars," by Robert Wallace, and what was the name of the program that presented it?
2. The history of aviation was a documentary series entitled AIR POWER and was certainly well-received by the television viewing audience. Who was the host/narrator of this program?
3. One of television's earliest war drama series starred Michael Thomas and Cliff Clark, and was set in North Africa. What was the name of this program?
4. As unlikely as it seems, the principal character in this series was a mild mannered newspaper proofreader. name the program and the star.
5. A self-appointed judge who said he was "the law west of the Pecos" was the hero in this western series. Name the show and the star.
6. Ken Thurston, an American intelligence agent with the code name "X", was the lead character in an exciting series which began on radio, and then came to television. What was the name of the program and who played the television lead?
7. The Goose Bar Ranch was the setting for this

adventure series based on Mary O'Hara's book. What was the name of this series?

8. NBC's popular Sunday night COLGATE COMEDY HOUR was succeeded by THE NBC COMEDY HOUR, and initially had a permanent hostess. Who was she?

9. N.O.P.D. was the name of this crime drama series which starred Stacy Harris and Lou Sirgo. What did N.O.P.D. stand for, and what roles did these stars play?

10. An interesting medical drama series was produced by Jack Webb, centered around two veterinarians. Name the show and the stars.

11. The *SS Ocean Queen,* a cruise ship, was the setting for this comedy series which starred Gale Storm and featured ZaSu Pitts. What was the name of the show and what characters did Gale Storm and ZaSu Pitts play?

12. The adventures of the famous comic book character Red Ryder was brought to the television screen in a thirty-minute weekly series. Who played Red Ryder?

13. India during the late nineteenth century was the setting for this adventure series. The principal characters were Lieutenants Rhodes and Storn, and Colonel Standish. What was the name of the program and who were the stars?

14. Buddy Hackett and a now famous comedienne/ actress appeared in a situation comedy revolving around the episodes of a proprietor of a newsstand. Name the show and the comedienne.

15. The Box brothers, Harvey and Gilmore, owned and operated a photography studio in San Francisco. This situation comedy had to do with their various antics. What was the name of this series, and who were the stars?

16. Captain Dan Tempest, Commander of The Sultana, was hero of this adventure series on Saturday nights on the CBS network. What was the name of this program, and who played Dan Tempest?

17. A historical character was the hero of this western adventure series set in the Louisiana Territory of the 1830s. Name the program and star.

18. TO TELL THE TRUTH, the long-running popular game show premiered under another title. What was it?

19. NBC imported a swashbuckling adventure series from England set in the sixth and seventh centuries. Unfortunately, it was scheduled against THE BURNS AND ALLEN SHOW and MAKE ROOM FOR DADDY, and therefore, never had too much of a chance for success. Name the program and the star.

20. THE $64,000 CHALLENGE was a spinoff of the big money quiz show THE $64,000 QUESTION. Winners on the QUESTION were eligible to appear on CHALLENGE. Who was the original host and who followed him?

21. TWENTY-ONE was another of the big money quiz shows, and was indeed a very popular show. Fill in the following:
    A) What network was it on? _____
    B) On what day of the week was it originally aired? _____
    C) What was its initial time-slot? _____

22. Life at a military academy was the theme of this particular dramatic series. Name the show and the host.

23. Can you name the original host of a game show originally titled DO YOU TRUST YOUR WIFE? and later re-titled WHO DO YOU TRUST?

24. Dean Evans, Katherine Wells, and Dan Miller were three reporters working for Trans Globe News. This series depicted their experiences on a rotating basis. What was the name of the program, and who played the characters mentioned?

1957

1. The alluring Merle Oberon was the narrator and occasional performer in this adventure anthology about the exploits of the French Foreign Legion during World War II. Can you name this program?
2. A favorite comic strip character also popular with many movie fans; BLONDIE, the story of the Bumstead Family, began the first of its two short-running series in 1957. Who played Blondie and Dagwood in the first TV series?
3. The background for this western series was Fort Lowell and the Fifth Cavalry during the 1870s. What the name of the program?
4. Lyle Bettger played an investigator, and Paul Birch a defense attorney in this series about people who were falsely accused and even convicted of crimes for which they were innocent. Can you name this program?
5. Following her long association with OUR MISS BROOKS, Eve Arden embarked on another situation comedy series which was far less successful. In this series her occupation was that of a travelog lecturer. Name the character she played and what was the title of the show?

6. On what network did Frank Sinatra make his second attempt to provide a successful series?

7. An adventure show set during the Civil War about a Confederate soldier/spy who led daily raids against the Union Army starred Tod Andrews. Name the program and the principal character.

8. Captain David Scott and Jeff Kittridge were partners in a boat business on Scott Island in New England. _____ was the name of the program and _____ _____ and _____ _____ were the stars.

9. One of the few television programs to be among the top four rated shows during its first four seasons was a half-hour western. What was its name?

10. LEAVE IT TO BEAVER was a favorite comedy series for many years. Can you name the family members and who played them?

11. A Chicago plainclothes detective was the principal character in this police drama. Name the program, the character and who starred in the role.

12. A tough private eye with no first name was the hero in this detective series which initially ran on the NBC network. Can you name the series and the star?

13. Howard Duff and Ida Lupino played a film star couple in this series. (They were married to each other in real life at this time.) Name the program they starred in.

14. The Office of Strategic Services (O.S.S.), the American Intelligence Agency during World War II, was the background setting for this exciting war dramatic series. Captain Frank Hawthorn was the O.S.S. agent working behind enemy lines, and the character most stories revolved around. Who played this role, and what was the name of the program?

15. THE REAL McCOYS was television's first successful rural situation comedy and starred Academy Award-winner Walter Brennan in the role of Grandpa Amos McCoy. The grandson was played by an actor who went on to star in several series in the sixties and seventies. Name the actor.

16. Vint Bonner was a Civil War veteran who traveled throughout the West helping people in distress. Who was the actor who played this role and what was the name of the program?

17. Joan Caulfield starred in a comedy series about a former salesclerk who became the traveling companion of a weathy, slightly wacky widow on a trip around the world. Can you name the program and who played the widow?

18. _____ starred as State Trooper Rod Blake of the Nevada State Troopers.

19. The stories told in this series were from the actual files of the Texas Rangers. Hoby Gilman was the name of the ranger who was the principal character. What was the name of the program, and who was the actor?

20. A Sunday early evening program which was to be a fixture for many years was a documentary series that presented filmed reports of major events and personalities. Name the program and the narrator.

21. The Arizona Rangers provided the stories for this half-hour western series which had an unusual title. Can you remember it?

22. Long before he became the host of ABC's WIDE WORLD OF SPORTS, Jim McKay played a court reporter in a popular courtroom drama series. What was the name of that courtroom series?

23. TALES OF WELLS FARGO was a high-rated western series that ran on Monday nights for five years. Dale Robertson played the lead character. What was his name?

24. CALL MR. D was this show's name when it went into syndication. Under what title was it originally known?

1958

1. One of the West's most popular heros was William Bartley (Bat) Masterson. Gene Barry starred as Bat Masterson, Sheriff of Dodge City, who preferred to disarm his adversaries with his wits rather than his gun. What were his trademarks?
2. Tommy Nolan starred as ten-year-old Jody O'Connell in this series about life in the West, as seen through the eyes of a youngster. The setting for this program was in Montana. What was the name of this show?
3. CASEY JONES was an adventure series about the legendary railroad engineer of the famous Cannonball Express. Who played Casey Jones?
4. The cunning, shrewd, and level-headed Chinese detective CHARLIE CHAN and his number-one son, Barry, began a half-hour television mystery series this year. Who played Charlie Chan and who played his number-one son?
5. Matt Rockford, the town's ex-mayor, now a cattle rancher, was the leading character in this western adventure series. Can you name the program and who played Matt Rockford?
6. THE DONNA REED SHOW was a long time favorite situation comedy series on the ABC television net-

work. The stories were about the trials and tribulations of the _____ family living in the small town of _____.

7. HOW TO MARRY A MILLIONAIRE was a sitcom based on the motion picture about three New York career girls, each looking for a wealthy husband. Who were the original stars of this series?

8. A summer replacement detective series featured a son who was a private eye and his father, a former reporter, combining their talents to solve crimes. Can you name the program and stars?

9. IVANHOE, Sir Walter Scott's novel, was an adventure series filmed in England. Who was the star?

10. Jeff Richards played a crusading newspaper editor and publisher in the gold mining town of Jubilee during the 1850s. Even though he possessed a mighty pen he was equally proficient with a gun. Name this western series.

11. Charles Van Doren, college professor and popular winner in the quiz show TWENTY-ONE, hosted this Sunday afternoon series which alternated biweekly with OMNIBUS. Name the program.

12. Laramie, Wyoming was the setting for this series about Marshal Dan Troup and his Deputy Johnnie McKay, and their attempts to keep law and order. Who played the marshal, the deputy, and what was the name of the program?

13. Anne Jeffreys and Robert Sterling, married to each other in real life, and who previously appeared in TOPPER, teamed up again to star in another comedy series. This time they were owners of rival modeling agencies. Name the program and the actress who played Ginger, one of the models.

14. Mike Kovac was a freelance photographer who helped the police solve crimes. Who played Kovac and what was the name of the program?

15. Author Mickey Spillane's famous private detective character MIKE HAMMER became a television series in 1958. What actor played Mike Hammer?

16. NAKED CITY was a popular police drama series that

was actually filmed on location all over New York City. What was the famous tag line the narrator used at the end of the show?

17. An historical adventure series, set in the time of the French and Indian War (1754–1759), was about the search for a water route that would supposedly link the East and West. Can you name the program and who were the stars?

18. PETER GUNN, the suave, sophisticated private detective, hung out at a jazz nightclub called "Mother's." Who originally played Mother?

19. What was the name of the first drama series about the experiences of paramedics and who was the star?

20. THE RIFLEMAN was the story of Lucas McCain, played by Chuck Connors, and his son Mark, and the struggle to maintain their cattle ranch. Who played Mark McCain?

21. Milton Coniff's popular comic strip character STEVE CANYON was a one-season prime-time network adventure show. What network was it originally on and who starred as Steve Canyon?

22. Bill Longley was a fast gun, a wanderer and a friend to people in distress in Texas during the 1870s. What was the name of the western series in which he was the principal character and who played him?

23. YANCY DERRINGER, the legendary character was an ex-confederate soldier turned gambler and adventurer who worked as a special agent for the city administrator of New Orleans. Who starred in this role?

24. The experiences of two long-distance truckers working for the ITT Trucking Company was the story line for this half-hour adventure series. What was the name of the program and who were the stars?

1959

1. THE ALASKANS was an adventure series set during the Gold Rush of the 1890s. Silky Harris, Renn McKee and their beautiful singer friend Rocky Shaw were always trying to find a gold mine, but never did. Who were the stars of this show?
2. BONANZA'S patriarch Ben Cartwright was a three-time widower. Can you name his wives?
3. Cal Calhoun and Rex Randolph were two private detectives in this hour-long series set in New Orleans. Name the program and the stars.
4. A father and son, two generations of New York police officers, were the leading characters in this crime drama series. Name the program and the stars.
5. A fast-paced quiz show in which two colleges or universities competed for scholorship funds was titled COLLEGE BOWL. Can you name the first host of this show?
6. After having played cops on two previous series this actor played Dan Adams, private eye in this 1959 series. Who is the actor and what was the name of this program?
7. In this situation comedy Hal Towne was a widower and a newspaper columnist raising his ten-year-old

son in Los Angeles. Who starred as Hal Towne and what was the name of the show?

8. Jay North starred as Dennis Mitchell in DENNIS THE MENACE, the story of a mischievous young boy who was always trying to help out but usually made things worse. Who played Dennis' parents?

9. Marshall Simon Frey and his deputy Clay McCord were the "keepers of law and order" in Silver City, Arizona during the 1880s. Name the program and who played Frey and McCord.

10. The team of Captain Matt Holbrook, Lieutenants Johnny Russo, Joe Conway, and Otto Lindstrom made up the principal characters in the police drama titled THE DETECTIVES. Who were the members of the original cast?

11. You probably recall that Dwayne Hickman played Dobie Gillis in the show, THE MANY LOVES OF DOBIE GILLIS, but who played Herbert and Winifred (Winnie) Gillis, his parents?

12. FIBBER McGEE AND MOLLY was one of the most popular radio programs and was on for more than twenty years. On television it lasted only twenty-six episodes. Who played the television team of Fibber McGee and Molly?

13. HENNESEY was a comedy series starring Jackie Cooper as a Navy doctor stationed in San Diego. He was a likable guy who always had things happen to him and was constantly admonished by his Commanding Officer, Captain Wally Shafer. Who played Captain Shafer?

14. HOTEL DE PAREE was probably the strangest title for a Western series. The hotel was located in Georgetown, Colorado and owned by a legendary character, a gunfighter turned lawman. What was the legendary character's name and who played him?

15. New York City in the Roaring Twenties was the setting for this police drama. It was the first series to deal with the lawlessness, the gangsters, prohibition, etc, and based on the exploits of the real-life police

detective Barney Ruditsky. Name the program and the star.

16. The music publishing business was the background setting for this comedy series. William Demarest, Stubby Kaye and Murray Hamilton were some of the principal actors in the cast. What was the name of the program?

17. In this adventure series Dr. Glenn Barton was a government research scientist who was involved with experiments designed to measure the limits of human endurance. Who played Dr. Barton and what was the name of the series?

18. Occasionally, a western series would come along that was a little different. This one had as the hero not a lawman or gunfighter, or special government agent, but an insurance investigator. Can you name the program and star?

19. MANHUNT was a thirty-minute drama series in which a police officer and a police reporter combined their talents to solve crimes. Who were the stars of this program?

20. One of the few programs ever produced in cooperation with the Department of Defense had to do with the government's effort to further the space program. Each week the cast varied with the exception of Colonel Ed McCauley, who was the only regular cast member. What was the name of this science adventure series and who played Colonel McCauley?

21. MR. LUCKY, from the show of the same name, was a professional gambler who was the owner of a floating casino, The Fortuna. Episodes depicted him and his friend Andamo trying to run an honest operation. Who played Mr. Lucky and what actor portrayed Andamo?

22. Attorney Steve Peck was the father of a typical middle-class family. He had a wife, and children, and home in the suburbs. Torey Peck was his twelve-year-old mischievous little girl who always got herself into comical but troublesome situations. Can you

name the program and who played Steve and Torey Peck?

23. A detective series with a twist featured a private detective who was also a jazz pianist working at Waldo's, a Greenwich Village club. John Cassavetes played the title role. What was the name of the program?

24. Kodiack and Dugan was a team of construction supervisors/engineers who solved problems relating to building highways, dams, airports, skyscrapers, etc. What was the name of this adventure program and who were the stars?

Photo Album

Question 1:
It looks like the man in the middle was "taken."
How long was this series on network television?

Question 2:
Name this smiling cast.

61

Question 3:
This team was one of the most likable and durable in the history of show business. How many years were they together on network TV?

Question 4:
This cheerful couple were New Yorkers of an earlier generation. Who were they?

63

Question 5:
Who is the actor with the quizzical look and in what series did he star?

Question 6:
The man in the chair must be telling an interesting story. Do you know who he is and in what dramatic series he appeared?

Question 7:
Miss Kitty always had "eyes" for Marshal Dillon. Name the saloon she owned and her surname.

Question 8:
Can you remember the original name of this comedy series?

Question 9:
**Ernie Bilko was always a winner. What was the
original name of his comedy series?**

Question 10:
This knight in black was always available to fight against injustice. Where did he live?

Question 11:
There was always a lot of serious conversation going on at this table. Who's missing?

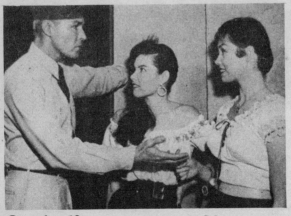

Question 12:
Little did this handsome officer realize at that time what a great future star (girl on far right) he was talking to. Name the character he's playing and who is the actress on the right?

Question 13:
This is the captain and his original crew. Name
the program.

Question 14:
Even though they're smiling they did not last more
than one season on network television. What program were these characters in?

Question 15:
You couldn't keep this man out of the water. Who is the character portrayed and what was the name of the weekly adventure series he was in?

Prime-Time
Network Program
Schedules

		7PM	7:30	8PM	8:30
Sunday	ABC	Paul Whiteman Revue	Showtime USA	Hollywood Premiere Theater	Sit or Miss
	CBS	Gene Autry	This is Show Business	Toast of the Town	
	NBC	Leave It To The Girls		Colgate Comedy Hour	
Monday	ABC	Club Seven	Hollywood Screen Test	Treasury Men in Action	Dick Tracy
	CBS	Stork Club	Perry Como	Lux Video Theater	Arthur Godfrey's Talent Scouts
	NBC	Kukla, Fran and Ollie	Mohawk Showroom	Paul Winchell	Voice of Firestone
Tuesday	ABC	Club Seven	Beulah	Football Game of the Week	Buck Rogers
	CBS	Stork Club	Faye Emerson	Prudential Family Playhouse/ Sure as Fate	
	NBC	Kukla, Fran and Ollie	Little Show	The Texaco Star Theater (The Milton Berle Show)	
Wednesday	ABC	Club Seven	Chance of A Lifetime	First Nighter	
	CBS	Stork Club	Perry Como	Arthur Godfrey and His Friends	
	NBC	Kukla, Fran and Ollie	Mohawk Showroom	Four Star Revue	
Thursday	ABC	Club Seven	Lone Ranger	Stop the Music	
	CBS	Stork Club	Faye Emerson	Show Goes On	
	NBC	Kukla, Fran and Ollie	Mohawk Showroom	You Bet Your Life	
Friday	ABC	Club Seven	Life with Linkletter	Twenty Questions	Pro Football Highlights
	CBS	Stork Club	Perry Como	Mama	Man Against Crime
	NBC	Kukla, Fran and Ollie	Mohawk Showroom	Quiz Kids	We The People
Saturday	ABC	Sandy Dreams	Stu Erwin Show	Paul Whiteman's TV Teen Club	
	CBS	Big Top	Week in Review / Faye Emerson	Ken Murray Show	
	NBC	Hank McCune	One Man's Family	Jack Carter Show	

Question 1:
TWENTY QUESTIONS, the popular quiz show, was hosted by _____ _____ .

NETWORK
SCHEDULE

9PM	9:30	10PM	10:30	11PM	
Soap Box Derby	Marshall Plan in Action	Old Fashioned Meeting	Youth on The March	ABC	Sunday
Fred Waring Show		Celebrity Time	What's My Line	CBS	
Philco Television Playhouse		Garroway At Large	Take A Chance	NBC	
College Bowl	On Trial	Movie		ABC	Monday
Horace Heidt Show	The Goldbergs	Studio One		CBS	
Lights Out	Robert Montgomery Presents/ Musical Comedy Time		Who Said That	NBC	
Billy Rose Show	Can You Top This	Life Begins At Eighty	Roller Derby	ABC	Tuesday
Vaughn Monroe	Suspense	Danger	We Take Your Word	CBS	
Fireside Theater	Armstrong Circle Theater	Ted Mack's Original Amateur Hour		NBC	
Don McNeill TV Club		Wrestling		ABC	Wednesday
Somerset Maugham Theater	The Web	Pabst Blue Ribbon Bouts		CBS	
Kraft Television Theater		Break The Bank	Stars over Hollywood	NBC	
Holiday Hotel	Blind Date	I Cover Times Square	Roller Derby	ABC	Thursday
Alan Young Show	Big Town	Truth or Consequences	NASA Airflyers Theater	CBS	
Kay Kyser's Kollege of Musical Knowledge		Martin Kane	Wayne King	NBC	
Pulitzer Prize Play House		PentHouse Party	Stud's Place	ABC	Friday
Ford Theater/ Magnavox Theater		Star of The Family	Beat The Clock	CBS	
Versatile Varieties	Big Stokey/ The Clock	Gillette Cavalcade of Sports		NBC	
Roller Derby				ABC	Saturday
Frank Sinatra Show		Sing It Again		CBS	
Your Show of Shows		Your Hit Parade		NBC	

		7PM	7:30PM	8PM	8:30
Sunday	ABC	Paul Whiteman's Revue	Music in Velvet	Movie	
	CBS	Gene Autry	This is Show Business	Toast of The Town	
	NBC	Chesterfield Sound Off Time	Young Mr. Bobbin	Colgate Comedy Time	
Monday	ABC		Hollywood Screen Test		Life Begins at Eighty
	CBS		Perry Como	Lux Video Theater	Arthur Godfrey's Talent Scouts
	NBC	Kukla, Fran and Ollie	Mohawk Showroom	Paul Winchell	Voice of Firestone
Tuesday	ABC		Beulah	Charlie Wild	How Did They Get That Way
	CBS		Stork Club	Frank Sinatra Show	
	NBC	Kukla, Fran and Ollie	Little Show	The Texaco Star Theater (The Milton Berle Show)	
Wednesday	ABC		Chance of A Lifetime	Paul Dixon Show	
	CBS		Perry Como	Arthur Godfrey & His Friends	
	NBC	Kukla, Fran and Ollie	Mohawk Showroom	Kate Smith Evening Hour	
Thursday	ABC		Lone Ranger	Stop The Music	
	CBS		Stork Club	Burns and Allen/ Garry Moore Show	Amos "n" Andy
	NBC	Kukla, Fran and Ollie	Little Show	You Bet Your Life	Treasury Men in Action
Friday	ABC		Life with Linkletter/ Say it with Acting	Mark Saber	Stu Erwin Show
	CBS		Perry Como	Mama	Man Against Crime
	NBC	Kukla, Fran and Ollie	Mohawk Showroom	Quiz Kids	We The People
Saturday	ABC	Hollywood Theater Time		Paul Whiteman's Teen Club	
	CBS	Sammy Kaye Show	Beat The Clock	Ken Murray Show	
	NBC	American Youth Forum	One Man's Family	All Star Revue	

Question 2:

___ _____ was Arthur Godfrey's announcer on
TALENT SCOUTS.

74

NETWORK SCHEDULE

9PM	9:30	10PM	10:30	11PM		
	Marshall Plan in Action	Hour of Decision	Youth on The March	ABC	Sunday
Fred Waring Show		Celebrity Time	What's My Line	CBS	
Philco TV Playhouse/ Good Year TV Playhouse		Red Skelton Show	Leave It To The Girls	NBC	
Curtain Up		Bill Gwinn Show	Studs Place	ABC	Monday
I Love Lucy	It's News To Me	Studio One		CBS	
Lights Out	Robert Montgomery Presents/ Somerset Maugham TV Theater			NBC	
United or Not	On Trial		Actors Hotel	ABC	Tuesday
Crime Syndicated	Suspense	Danger		CBS	
Fireside Theater	Armstrong Circle Theater	Ted Mack's Original Amateur Hour		NBC	
Don McNeill TV Club/ Arthur Murray Party	The Clock	Celanese Theater/ King Crossroads		ABC	Wednesday
Strike It Rich	The Web	Pabst Blue Ribbon Bouts		CBS	
Kraft Television Theater		Break The Bank	Freddy Martin Show	NBC	
Herb Shriner Show	Gruen Guild Theater	Paul Dixon Show	Masland at Home Show / Carmel Myers Show	ABC	Thursday
Alan Young Show	Big Town	Racket Squad	Crime Photographer	CBS	
Ford Festival		Martin Kane	Wayne King	NBC	
Crime with Father	Versatile Varieties/ Tales of Tomorrow	Dell O'Dell Show	America in View	ABC	Friday
Schlitz Playhouse of Stars		Live Like A Millionaire	Hollywood Opening Night	CBS	
Big Story	Aldrich Family	Gillette Cavalcade of Sports		NBC	
Lesson in Safety	American Health			ABC	Saturday
Faye Emerson's Wonderful Town	The Show Goes on	Songs for Sale		CBS	
	Your Show of Shows		Your Hit Parade	NBC	

75

		7PM	7:30	8PM	8:30
Sunday	ABC	You Asked For It	Hot Seat	All-Star News	
	CBS	Gene Autry	This is Show Business	Toast of the Town	
	NBC	Red Skelton Show	Doc Corkle	Colgate Comedy Hour	
Monday	ABC		Hollywood Screen Test	Mark Saber	United or Not
	CBS		Perry Como	Lux Video Theater	Arthur Godfrey's Talent Scouts
	NBC		Those Two	Paul Winchell	Voice of Firestone
Tuesday	ABC		Beulah		
	CBS		Heaven for Betsy	Leave It to Larry	Red Buttons
	NBC		Dinah Shore	The Texaco Star Theater (The Milton Berle Show)	
Wednesday	ABC		Names The Same	All Star News	
	CBS		Perry Como	Arthur Godfrey & His Friends	
	NBC		Those Two	I Married Joan	Scott Music Hall/ Cavalcade of America
Thursday	ABC		Lone Ranger	All Star News	Chance of A Lifetime
	CBS		Heaven for Betsy	Burns & Allen Show	Amos "n" Andy/ Four Star Playhouse
	NBC		Dinah Shore	You Bet Your Life	Treasury Men in Action
Friday	ABC		Stu Erwin Show	Ozzie and Harriet	All Star
	CBS		Perry Como	Mama	My Friend Irma
	NBC		Those Two	RCA Victor Show	Gulf Playhouse
Saturday	ABC	Paul Whitman's TV Teen Club	Live Like A Millionaire	Film Playhouse	
	CBS		Beat The Clock	Jackie Gleason Show	
	NBC	Mr. Wizard	My Little Margie	All-Star Revue	

Question 3:
HOUR OF DECISION was what type of program?

NETWORK SCHEDULE

9PM	9:30	10PM	10:30	11PM		
Playhouse #7	This is the Life	Hour of Decision	Anywhere USA		ABC	Sunday
Fred Waring Show	Break the Bank	The Web	What's My Line		CBS	Sunday
Philco TV Playhouse/ Goodyear TV Playhouse		The Doctor			NBC	Sunday
All-Star News					ABC	Monday
I Love Lucy	Life with Luigi	Studio One			CBS	Monday
Hollywood Opening Night	Robert Montgomery Presents		Who Said That		NBC	Monday
					ABC	Tuesday
Crime Syndicated/ City Hospital	Suspense	Danger			CBS	Tuesday
Fireside Theater	Armstrong Circle Theater	Two For The Money	Club Embassey	On Life with Considine	NBC	Tuesday
Adventures of Ellery Queen		Wrestling			ABC	Wednesday
Strike It Rich	Man Against Crime	Pabst Blue Ribbon Bouts			CBS	Wednesday
Kraft Television Theater		This Is Your Life			NBC	Wednesday
Perspective	On Guard				ABC	Thursday
Pick Dat Winner	Big Town	Racket Squad	I've Got a Secret		CBS	Thursday
Dragnet/ Gangbusters	Ford Theater	Martin Kane			NBC	Thursday
News	Tales of Tomorrow				ABC	Friday
Schlitz Playhouse	Our Miss Brooks	Mr & Mrs North			CBS	Friday
Big Story	Aldrich Family	Gillette Cavalcade of Sports			NBC	Friday
Film Playhouse					ABC	Saturday
Jane Froman's U.S.A. Canteen	Meet Millie	Balance Your Budget	Battle of the Ages		CBS	Saturday
Your Show of Shows			Your Hit Parade		NBC	Saturday

		7PM	7:30	8PM	8:30
Sunday	ABC	You Asked for It	Frank Leahy Show	Notre Dame Football	
	CBS	Quiz Kids	Jack Benny Show/ Private Secretary	Toast of the Town	
	NBC	Paul Winchell Show	Mr. Peepers	Colgate Comedy Hour	
Monday	ABC	Walter Winchell	Jamie	Sky King	Of Many Things
	CBS		Perry Como	Burns & Allen	Arthur Godfrey's Talent Scouts
	NBC		Arthur Murray Part	Name That Tune	Voice of Firestone
Tuesday	ABC		Cavalcade of America		
	CBS		Jane Froman	Gene Autry	Red Skelton Show
	NBC		Dinah Shore	Buck Berle Show	
Wednesday	ABC		Inspector Mark Saber	At Issue / Through the Curtain	America in View
	CBS		Perry Como	Arthur Godfrey & His Friends	
	NBC		Coke Time	I Married Joan	My Little Margie
Thursday	ABC		Lone Ranger	Quick as a Flash	Where's Raymond
	CBS		Jane Froman	Meet Mr. McNutley	Four Star Playhouse
	NBC		Dinah Shore	You Bet Your Life	Treasury Men in Action
Friday	ABC		Stu Erwin Show	Ozzie & Harriet	Pepsi-Cola Playhouse
	CBS		Perry Como	Mama	Topper
	NBC		Coke Time	Dave Garroway Show	Life of Riley
Saturday	ABC	Paul Whiteman's TV Teen Club	Leave it to the Girls	Talent Patrol	Music at the Meadowbrook
	CBS	Meet Millie	Beat the Clock	Jackie Gleason Show	
	NBC	Mr. Wizard	Ethel & Albert	Bonino	Ted Mack's Original Amateur Hour

Question 4:
TWO FOR THE MONEY was hosted by _____ _____.

NETWORK
SCHEDULE

9PM		9:30	10PM	10:30	11PM	
Walter Winchell Show	Orchid Award	Peter Potter Show		Hour of Decision	ABC	Sunday
G. E. Theater/ Fred Waring Show		Man Behind the Badge	The Web	What's My Line	CBS	
Philco TV Playhouse/ Goodyear TV Playhouse			Letter to Loretta	Man Against Crime	NBC	
Junior Press Conference		Big Picture	This is the Life		ABC	Monday
I Love Lucy		Red Buttons Show	Studio One		CBS	
RCA Victor Show Starring Dennis Day		Robert Montgomery Presents		Who Said That	NBC	
Make Room for Daddy		U.S. Steel Hour/Motorola TV Theater		Name's the Same	ABC	Tuesday
This is Show Business		Suspense	Danger	See It Now	CBS	
Fireside Theatre		Armstrong Circle Theatre	Judge for Yourself	On the Line with Considine / It Happened In Sports	NBC	
Wrestling					ABC	Wednesday
Strike It Rich		I've Got a Secret	Pabst Blue Ribbon Bouts	Sports Spot	CBS	
Kraft Television Theatre			This Is Your Life		NBC	
Back That Fact		Kraft Television Theatre			ABC	Thursday
Lux Video Theatre		Big Town	Phillip Morris Playhouse	Place the Face	CBS	
Dragnet		Ford Theatre	Martin Kane		NBC	
Pride of the Family		Comeback Story	Showcase Theatre		ABC	Friday
Schlitz Playhouse		Our Miss Brooks	My Friend Irma	Person to Person	CBS	
Big Story		Campbell Soundstage	Gillette Cavalcade of Sports	Greatest Fights	NBC	
Saturday Night Fights		Fight Talk	Madison Square Garden Highlights		ABC	Saturday
Two for the Money		My Favorite Husband	Medallion Theatre	Revlon Mirror Theatre	CBS	
Your Show of Shows				Your Hit Parade	NBC	

		7PM	7:30	8PM	8:30
Sunday	ABC	You Asked For It	Pepsi Cola Playhouse	Flight #7	Big Picture
	CBS	Lassie	Jack Benny Show/ Private Secretary	Toast of the Town	
	NBC	People Are Funny	Mr. Peepers	Colgate Comedy Hour	
Monday	ABC	Kukla, Fran and Ollie	Name's The Same	Come Closer	Voice of Firestone
	CBS		Perry Como	Burns and Allen Show	Arthur Godfrey's Talent Scouts
	NBC		Tony Martin	Caesar's Hour	
Tuesday	ABC	Kukla, Fran and Ollie	Cavalcade of America		Twenty Questions
	CBS		Jo Stafford	Red Skelton Show	Halls of Ivy
	NBC		Dinah Shore	Buick Berle Show	
Wednesday	ABC	Kukla, Fran and Ollie	Disneyland		Stu Erwin Show
	CBS		Perry Como	Arthur Godfrey and His Friends	
	NBC		Coke Time	I Married Joan	My Little Margie
Thursday	ABC	Kukla, Fran and Ollie	Lone Ranger	Mail Story	Treasury Man in Action
	CBS		Jane Froman	Ray Milland Show	Climax
	NBC		Dinah Shore	You Bet Your Life	Justice
Friday	ABC	Kukla, Fran and Ollie	Adventures of Rin Tin Tin	Ozzie and Harriet	Ray Bolger Show
	CBS		Perry Como	Mama	Topper
	NBC		Coke Time	Red Buttons	Life of Riley
Saturday	ABC		Compass	Dotty Mack Show	
	CBS	Gene Autry	Beat The Clock	Jackie Gleason Show	
	NBC	Mr. Wizard	Ethel & Albert	Mickey Rooney	Place The Face

Question 5:
Name the host of DOLLAR A SECOND.

NETWORK SCHEDULE

9PM	9:30	10PM	10:30	11PM	Network	Day
Walter Winchell Show	Martha Wright Show	Dr I.Q.	Break The Bank		ABC	Sunday
G.E. Theater	Honestly Celeste	Father Knows Best	What's My Line		CBS	Sunday
Philco TV Playhouse/Goodyear TV Playhouse		Loretta Young Show	The Hunter		NBC	Sunday
Junior Press Conference		Boxing			ABC	Monday
I Love Lucy	December Bride	Studio One			CBS	Monday
Medic	Robert Montgomery Presents				NBC	Monday
Make Room For Daddy	U.S. Steel Hour/Elgin TV Hour		Stop The Music		ABC	Tuesday
Meet Millie	Danger	Life With Father	See It Now		CBS	Tuesday
Fireside Theater	Armstrong Circle Theater	Truth or Consequences	It's A Great Life		NBC	Tuesday
Masquerade Party	Enterprise				ABC	Wednesday
Strike It Rich	I've Got A Secret	Pabst Blue Ribbon Bouts			CBS	Wednesday
Kraft Television Theater		This Is Your Life	Big Town		NBC	Wednesday
So You Want to Lead A Band	Kraft Television Theater				ABC	Thursday
Climax	Four Star Playhouse	Public Defender	Name That Tune		CBS	Thursday
Dragnet	Ford Theater	Lux Video Theater			NBC	Thursday
Dollar A Second	The Vise				ABC	Friday
Schlitz Playhouse	Our Miss Brooks	The Lineup	Person to Person		CBS	Friday
Big Story	Dear Phoebe	Gillette Cavalcade of Sports			NBC	Friday
Saturday Night Fights		Stork Club			ABC	Saturday
Two For The Money	My Favorite Husband	That's My Boy	Willy		CBS	Saturday
Imogene Coca Show	Jimmy Durante Show/Donald O'Conner Sho	George Gobel Show	Your Hit Parade		NBC	Saturday

		7PM	7:30	8PM	8:30
Sunday	ABC	You Asked For It		Famous Film Festival	
	CBS	Lassie	Jack Benny Show/ Private Secretary	The Ed Sullivan Show	
	NBC	It's A Great Life	Frontier	Colgate Variety Hour	
Monday	ABC	Kukla, Fran and Ollie	Topper	TV Readers Digest	Voice of Firestone
	CBS		Adventures of Robin Hood	Burns and Allen Show	Arthur Godfrey's Talent Scouts
	NBC		Tony Martin Show	Caesar's Hour	
Tuesday	ABC	Kukla, Fran and Ollie	Warner Brother Presents		Wyatt Earp
	CBS		Name That Tune	Navy Log	You'll Never Get Rich
	NBC		Dinah Shore Show	The Chevy Show (Milton Berle, Martha Raye, Bob Hope)	
Wednesday	ABC	Kukla, Fran and Ollie	Disneyland		MGM Parade
	CBS		Brave Eagle	Arthur Godfrey & His Friends	
	NBC		Coke Time	Screen Director Playhouse	Father Knows Best
Thursday	ABC	Kukla, Fran and Ollie	Lone Ranger	Bishop Sheen	Stop The Music
	CBS		Sgt Preston of The Yukon	Love That Bob	Climax
	NBC		Dinah Shore Show	You Bet Your Life	People's Choice
Friday	ABC	Kukla, Fran and Ollie	Adventures of Rin Tin Tin	Ozzie and Harriet	Crossroads
	CBS		Adventures of Champion	Mama	Our Miss Brooks
	NBC		Coke Time	Truth or Consequences	Life of Riley
Saturday	ABC			Ozark Jubilee	
	CBS	Gene Autry	Beat The Clock	Stage Show	The Honeymooners
	NBC		Big Surprise	Perry Como Show	

Question 6:
_____ _____ *was the emcee on CHANCE OF A LIFE-
TIME.*

NETWORK SCHEDULE

9PM	9:30	10PM	10:30	11PM	
Chance of A Lifetime	Ted Mack's Original Amateur Hour	Life Begins At Eighty		ABC	Sunday
G.E. Theater	Alfred Hitchcock	Appointment With Adventure	What's My Line	CBS	
Goodyear TV Playhouse/ Alcoa Hour		Loretta Young Show	Justice	NBC	
Dotty Mack Show	Medical Horizon	Big Picture		ABC	Monday
I Love Lucy	December Bride	Studio One		CBS	
Medic	Robert Montgomery Presents			NBC	
Make Room For Daddy	Dupont Cavalcade Theater	Talent Varieties		ABC	Tuesday
Meet Millie	Red Skelton Show	$64,000 Question	My Favorite Husband	CBS	
Fireside Theater	Armstrong Circle Theater/ Pontiac Presents Playwrights '56		Big Town	NBC	
Masquerade Party	Break The Bank	Wednesday Night Fights		ABC	Wednesday
The Millionaire	I've Got A Secret	20th Century Fox Hour/ U.S. Steel Hour		CBS	
Kraft Television Theater		This Is Your Life	Midwestern Hayride	NBC	
Star Tonight	Down You Go	Outside U.S.A.		ABC	Thursday
Climax	Four Star Playhouse	Johnny Carson Show	Wanted	CBS	
Dragnet	Ford Theater	Lux Video Theater		NBC	
Dollar A Second	The Vise	Ethel & Albert		ABC	Friday
The Crusader	Schlitz Playhouse	The Line Up	Person to Person	CBS	
Big Story	Star Stage	Gillette Cavalcade of Sports		NBC	
Lawrence Welk Show		Tomorrow's Careers		ABC	Saturday
Two For The Money	It's Always Jan	Gunsmoke	Damon Runyon Theater	CBS	
People are Funny	Jimmy Durante	George Gobel Show	Your Hit Parade	NBC	

		7PM	7:30	8PM	8:30
Sunday	ABC	You Asked For It	Ted Mack's Original Amateur Hour		Press Conference
	CBS	Lassie	Jack Benny Show/ Private Secretary	The Ed Sullivan Show	
	NBC	77th Bengal Lancers	Circus Boy	Steve Allen Show	
Monday	ABC	Kukla, Fran and Ollie	Bold Journey	Danny Thomas Show	Voice of Firestone
	CBS		Adventures of Robin Hood	Burns & Allen Show	Arthur Godfrey's Talent Scouts
	NBC		Nat "King" Cole Show	Adventures of Sir Lancelot	Stanley
Tuesday	ABC		Cheyenne/Conflict		Wyatt Earp
	CBS		Name That Tune	Phil Silvers Show	The Brothers
	NBC		Jonathan Winters Show	Big Surprise	Noah's Ark
Wednesday	ABC		Disneyland		Navy Log
	CBS		Giant Step	Arthur Godfrey Show	
	NBC		Eddie Fisher Show	Adventures of Hiram Holiday	Father Knows Best
Thursday	ABC		Lone Ranger	Circus Time	
	CBS		Sgt Preston of The Yukon	Love That Bob	Climax
	NBC		Dinah Shore Show	You Bet Your Life	Dragnet
Friday	ABC		Adventures of Rin Tin Tin	Jim Bowie	Crossroads
	CBS		My Friend Flicka	West Point Story	Zane Grey Theater
	NBC		Eddie Fisher Show	Life of Riley	Walter Winchell Show
Saturday	ABC		Famous Film Festival		
	CBS		The Buccaneers	Jackie Gleason Show	
	NBC		People Are Funny	Perry Como Show	

Question 7:
GIANT STEP, the prime-time game show for high school students, was hosted by _____ _____.

NETWORK SCHEDULE

9PM	9:30	10PM	10:30	11PM		
Omnibus					ABC	Sunday
G.E. Theater	Alfred Hitchcock	$64,000 Challenge	What's My Line		CBS	
Goodyear TV Playhouse/Alcoa Hour		Loretta Young Show	National Bowling Champions		NBC	
Bishop Sheen	Lawrence Welk Talent Show				ABC	Monday
I Love Lucy	December Bride	Studio One			CBS	
Medic	Robert Montgomery Presents				NBC	
Broken Arrow	Dupont Theater	It's Polka Time			ABC	Tuesday
Herb Shriner Show	Red Skelton Show	$64,000 Question	Do You Trust Your Wife		CBS	
Jane Wyman Show	Armstrong Circle Theater/Kaiser Aluminum Hour		Break The $250,000 Bank		NBC	
Ozzie and Harriet	Ford Theater	Wednesday Night Fights			ABC	Wednesday
The Millionaire	I've Got A Secret	20th Century Fox Hour/U.S. Steel Hour			CBS	
Kraft Television Theater		This is Your Life	Twenty-One		NBC	
Wire Service		Ozark Jubilee			ABC	Thursday
Climax		Playhouse 90			CBS	
Peoples Choice	Tennessee Ernie Ford	Lux Video Theater			NBC	
Treasury Hunt	The Vise	Ray Anthony Show			ABC	Friday
The Crusader	Schlitz Playhouse	The Line Up	Person to Person		CBS	
On Trial	Big Story	Gillette Cavalcade of Sports			NBC	
Lawrence Welk Show		Masquerade Party			ABC	Saturday
Gale Storm Show	Hey Jeannie	Gunsmoke	High Finance		CBS	
Caeser's Hour		George Gobel Show	Your Hit Parade		NBC	

		7PM	7:30	8PM	8:30
Sunday	ABC	You Asked For It	Maverick		Bowling Stars
	CBS	Lassie	Jack Benny Show/ Bachelor Father	The Ed Sullivan Show	
	NBC	Ted Mack's Original Amateur Hour	Sally	Steve Allen Show	
Monday	ABC		American Bandstand	Guy Mitchell Show	Bold Journey
	CBS		Robin Hood	Burns and Allen Show	Arthur Godfrey's Talent Scouts
	NBC		Price is Right	Restless Gun	Tales of Wells Fargo
Tuesday	ABC	Cheyenne/Sugarfoot			Wyatt Earp
	CBS		Name That Tune	Phil Silvers Show	Eve Arden Show
	NBC		Nat "King" Cole Show	Eddie Fisher Show/ George Gobel Show	
Wednesday	ABC	Disneyland			Tombstone Territory
	CBS		I Love Lucy	The Big Record	
	NBC		Wagon Train		Father Knows Best
Thursday	ABC		Circus Boy	Zorro	Real McCoys
	CBS		Sgt. Preston of the Yukon	Harbour Master	Climax
	NBC		Tic Tac Dough	You Bet Your Life	Dragnet
Friday	ABC		Adventures of Rin Tin Tin	Jim Bowie	Patrice Munsel Show
	CBS		Leave It To Beaver	Track Down	Zane Grey Theater
	NBC		Saber of London	Court of Last Resort	Life of Riley
Saturday	ABC		Keep It In The Family	Country Music Jubilee	
	CBS		Perry Mason		Dick & The Duchess
	NBC		People Are Funny	Perry Como Show	

Question 8:
ZORRO, the masked Spanish hero was played by
_____ _____ .

NETWORK
SCHEDULE

9PM	9:30	10PM	10:30	11PM	
Open Hearing	Football Game of the Week			ABC	Sunday
G.E. Theater	Alfred Hitchcock	$64,000 Challenge	What's My Line	CBS	
Dinah Shore Chevy Show		Loretta Young Show		NBC	
Voice of Firestone	Lawrence Welk Top Tunes and New Talent Show			ABC	Monday
Danny Thomas Show	December Bride	Studio One		CBS	
Twenty One	Goodyear Theater/ Alcoa Theater	Suspicion		NBC	
Broken Arrow	Telephone Time	West Point Story		ABC	Tuesday
To Tell The Truth	Red Skelton Show	$64,000 Question	Assignment Foreign Legion	CBS	
Meet McGraw	Love That Bob	The Californians		NBC	
Ozzie and Harriet	Walter Winchell File	Wednesday Night Fights		ABC	Wednesday
The Millionaire	I've Got A Secret	Armstrong Circle Theater/ U.S. Steel Hour		CBS	
Kraft Television Theater		This is Your Life		NBC	
Pat Boone Show	.O.S.S.	Navy Log		ABC	Thursday
Climax		Playhouse 90		CBS	
People's Choice	Tennessee Ernie Ford	Lux Show Starring Rosemary Clooney	Jane Wyman Theater	NBC	
Frank Sinatra Show	Date with The Angels	Colt 45		ABC	Friday
Mr Adams & Eve	Schlitz Playhouse	The Line Up	Person to Person	CBS	
M Squad	The Thin Man	Gillette Cavalcade of Sports		NBC	
Lawrence Welk Show		Mike Wallace Interviews		ABC	Saturday
Gale Storm Show	Have Gun, Will Travel	Gunsmoke		CBS	
Polly Bergen Show/ Club Oasis	Gisele MacKenzie Show	What's It For	Your Hit Parade	NBC	

87

		7PM	7:30	8PM	8:30
Sunday	ABC	You Asked For It	Maverick		The Lawman
	CBS	Lassie	Jack Benny Show/ Bachelor Father	The Ed Sullivan Show	
	NBC	Saber of London	Northwest Passage	Steve Allen Show	
Monday	ABC		Jubilee USA		Bold Journey
	CBS		Name That Tune	The Texan	Father Knows Best
	NBC		Tic Tac Dough	Restless Gun	Tales of Wells Fargo
Tuesday	ABC		Cheyenne/Sugarfoot		Wyatt Earp
	CBS		Stars in Action	Keep Talking	To Tell The Truth
	NBC		Dragnet	George Gobel Show/Eddie Fisher Show	
Wednesday	ABC		Lawrence Welk Show		Ozzie and Harriet
	CBS		Twilight Theater	Pursuit	
	NBC		Wagon Train		Price is Right
Thursday	ABC		Leave It To Beaver	Zorro	Real McCoys
	CBS		I Love Lucy	December Bride	Yancy Derringer
	NBC		Jefferson Drum	Ed Wynn Show	Twenty-one
Friday	ABC		Adventures of Rin Tin Tin	Walt Disney Presents	
	CBS		Your Hit Parade	Trackdown	Jackie Gleason Show
	NBC		Buckskin	Adventures of Ellery Queen	
Saturday	ABC		Dick Clark Show	Jubilee U.S.A.	
	CBS		Perry Mason		Wanted: Dead or Alive
	NBC		People are Funny	Perry Como Show	

Question 9:
Today, he's a sports commentator; back then he was the emcee of TIC TAC DOUGH. Who is he?

NETWORK SCHEDULE

9PM	9:30	10PM	10:30	11PM	
Colt 45		Encounter		ABC	Sunday
G.E. Theater	Alfred Hitchcock	$64,000 Question	What's My Line	CBS	
Dinah Shore Chevy Show		Loretta Young Show		NBC	
Voice of Firestone	Anybody Can Play	This Is Music		ABC	Monday
Danny Thomas Show	Ann Sothern Show	Desilu Playhouse		CBS	
Peter Gunn	Alcoa/Goodyear TV Playhouse	Arthur Murray Party		NBC	
The Rifleman	Naked City	Confession		ABC	Tuesday
Arthur Godfrey Show	Red Skelton Show	Garry Moore Show		CBS	
George Burns Show	Bob Cummings Show	The Californians		NBC	
Donna Reed Show	Patti Page Show	Wednesday Night Fights		ABC	Wednesday
The Millionaire	I've Got A Secret	Armstrong Circle Theater/U.S. Steel Hour		CBS	
Milton Berle in The Kraft Music Hall	Bat Masterson	This Is Your Life		NBC	
Pat Boone Show	Rough Riders	Traffic Court		ABC	Thursday
Zane Grey Theater		Playhouse 90		CBS	
Behind Closed Doors	Tennessee Ernie Ford	You Bet Your Life	Masquerade Party	NBC	
Man with A Camera		77 Sunset Strip		ABC	Friday
Phil Silvers Show	Lux Playhouse/ Schlitz Playhouse	The Line Up	Person to Person	CBS	
M Squad	Thin Man	Gillette Cavalcade of Sports		NBC	
Lawrence Welk		Sammy Kaye's Music		ABC	Saturday
Gale Storm Show	Have Gun, Will Travel	Gunsmoke		CBS	
Steve Canyon		Cimarron City	Brains and Brawn	NBC	

89

		7PM	7:30	8PM	8:30
Saturday	ABC	Colt 45		Maverick	The Lawman
	CBS	Lassie		Dennis The Menace	The Ed Sullivan Show
	NBC		Riverboat	Sunday Showcase	
Friday	ABC			Cheyenne	Bourbon
	CBS		Masquerade Party	The Texan	Father Knows Best
	NBC		Richard Diamond	Love and Marriage	Tales of Wells Fargo
Thursday	ABC			Sugarfoot/Bronco	Wyatt Earp
	CBS			Dennis O'Keefe Show	Dobie Gillis
	NBC		Laramie		Fibber McGee and Molly
Wednesday	ABC		Court of Last Resort	Hobby Lobby Show	Ozzie and Harriet
	CBS		The Lineup		Men into Space
	NBC		Wagon Train		Price is Right
Tuesday	ABC		Gale Storm (Oh! Susanna)	Donna Reed Show	Real McCoys
	CBS		To Tell The Truth	Betty Hutton Show	Johnny Ringo
	NBC		Law of The Plainsman	Bat Masterson	Staccato
Monday	ABC		Walt Disney Presents		Man From Black Hawk
	CBS		Rawhide		Hotel De Paree
	NBC		People Are Funny	Troubleshooters	Bell Telephone
Sunday	ABC		Dick Clark Show	High Road	Leave It To Beaver
	CBS		Perry Mason		Wanted: Dead or Alive
	NBC		Bonanza		The Man and The Challenge

Question 10:
The music from the MR. LUCKY series became very popular. Who was the composer?

NETWORK
SCHEDULE

9PM	9:30	10PM	10:30	11PM		
The Rebel	The Alaskans		Dick Clark's World of Talent	ABC	Sunday	
G.E. Theater	Alfred Hitchcock	Jack Benny Show/ George Gobel Show	What's My Line	CBS		
Dinah Shore Chevy Show		Loretta Young Show		NBC		
Street Beat	Adventures in Paradise		Man with a Camera	ABC	Monday	
Danny Thomas Show	Ann Sothern Show	Hennesey	June Allyson	CBS		
Peter Gunn	Goodyear/Alcoa TV Playhouse	Steve Allen Show		NBC		
The Rifleman	Philip Marlow	One Step Beyond	Keep Talking	ABC	Tuesday	
Tightrope	The Red Skelton Show	Garry Moore Show		CBS		
Arthur Murray Party	Star Time			NBC		
Hawaiian Eye		Wednesday Night Fights		ABC	Wednesday	
The Millionaire	I've Got A Secret	Armstrong Circle Theater/ U.S. Steel Hour		CBS		
Perry Como's Kraft Music Hall		This Is Your Life	Wichita Town	NBC		
Pat Boone	The Untouchables		Take A Good Look	ABC	Thursday	
Zane Grey Theater	Playhouse 90/Big Party			CBS		
Bachelor Father	Tennessee Ernie Ford	You Bet Your Life	The Lawless Years	NBC		
77 Sunset Strip		The Detectives	Black Saddle	ABC	Friday	
Desilu Playhouse		Twilight Zone	Person to Person	CBS		
Hour/Specials	M Squad	Gillette Cavalcade of Sports	Jackpot Bowling	NBC		
Lawrence Welk Show		Jubilee U.S.A.		ABC	Saturday	
Mr. Lucky	Have Gun, Will Travel	Gunsmoke	Markham	CBS		
The Deputy	Five Fingers		It Could Be You	NBC		

91

ANSWERS

1950

1. Ethel Waters
2. Jack Sterling and Ed McMahon
3. BIG TOWN—Patrick McVey, Mary K. Wells
4. Morey Amsterdam
5. Virgina Ruth Egnor
6. Ken Dibbs
7. Bea Benaderet and Hal March
8. THE COLGATE COMEDY HOUR
9. THE COLLEGE BOWL — Chico Marx
10. DETECTIVE'S WIFE
11. THE FIRST HUNDRED YEARS
12. I COVER TIMES SQUARE — Harold Huber
13. THE PRUDENTIAL FAMILY PLAYHOUSE
14. RACKET SQUAD — Reed Hadley
15. ROOTIE KAZOOTIE — Todd Russell
16. SONGS FOR SALE — Jan Murray
17. Ed Kemmer, Terra I
18. School principal
19. Jack Lemmon — THAT WONDERFUL GUY

20. TOM CORBETT, SPACE CADET — Frankie Thomas
21. TREASURY MEN IN ACTION — Walter Greaza
22. Dorothy Kilgallen, Louie Untermeyer, Dr. Richard Hoffman, and Harold Hoffman (former Governor of New Jersey)
23. Progress Hornsby, Somerset Winterset, Giuseppe Marinara
24. YOU ASKED FOR IT — Art Baker

1951

1. Jack Lemmon — THE AD-LIBBERS
2. ALL AROUND THE TOWN — Buff Cobb
3. BOSTON BLACKIE — Kent Taylor
4. THE EGG AND I — Pat Kirkland and Frank Craven
5. John Daly, Walter Cronkite, and Quincy Howe
6. Major Del Conway — THE FLYING TIGERS
7. Paul Garratt — JAY JOSTYN
8. SATURDAY ROUNDUP — KERMIT MAYNARD
9. Kirby Grant — THE SONGBIRD
10. STRIKE IT RICH — Warren Hull
11. Vivian Blaine — THOSE TWO
12. Peggy Ann Gardner and Peggy French — TWO GIRLS NAMED SMITH
13. WHAT'S THE STORY — Walt Raney, Walter Kiernan, Al Capp, and John K. M. McCaffery
14. James Butler Hickok and Jingles P. Jones
15. SEARCH FOR TOMORROW and LOVE OF LIFE
16. Helen Hayes
17. A) Alvin Childress B) Spencer Williams C) Tim Moore D) Ernestine Wade
18. Judy Foster — A DATE WITH JUDY
19. Dr. Bergen Evans

20. CRIME PHOTOGRAPHER — Richard Carlyle
21. Lugene Sanders
22. Don Herbert
23. Jack Mahoney, Dick Jones
24. OUT THERE and TALES OF TOMORROW

1952

1. Sara Churchill
2. BIFF BAKER USA — Alan Hale Jr. and Randy Stewart
3. BOSS LADY — Lynn Barrie
4. Melville Ruick — CITY HOSPITAL
5. THE CONTINENTAL — Renzo Cesara
6. COWBOY G-MEN — Russell Hayden and Jackie Coogan
7. DANGEROUS ASSIGNMENT — Brian Donlevy
8. DEATH VALLEY DAYS — Stanley Andrews
9. HEAVEN FOR BETSY — Jack Lemmon and Cynthia Stone
10. Bart Adams/Barry Nelson
11. Elena Verdugo and Florence Halop
12. Science teacher — Jefferson Junior High School
13. Nancy Remington, school nurse — Patricia Benoit
14. MY FRIEND IRMA — Irma Peterson, Marie Wilson and Cathy Lewis
15. Thackery Realty, MY HERO, Robert Cummings
16. Red Buttons — "Ho! Ho! . . . Hee! Hee! . . . Ha! Ha!"
17. RENDEZVOUS — David McKay
18. UP TO PARR

19. Richard Rogers, Leonard Graves
20. A) Thorny Thornberry/ Don DeFore B) 822 Sycamore Road
21. Jack Lescoulie and Jim Fleming
22. Vito Scotti
23. Walter Denton — Richard Crenna
24. POLICE STORY

1953

1. BONINO — Conrad Janis
2. CITY DETECTIVE — Lieutenant Bart Grant
3. Colonel Humphrey Flack
4. I LED THREE LIVES — Herbert Philbrick
5. JAMIE — Jamie McHummer
6. JIMMY HUGHES, ROOKIE COP
7. THE LORETTA YOUNG SHOW
8. Danny Williams ...... Danny Thomas
   Margaret Williams .... Jean Hagen
   Terry Williams .... Sherry Jackson
   Rusty Williams .... Rusty Hamer
9. THE MAN BEHIND THE BADGE — Charles Bickford
10. Joan Caulfield and Vanessa Brown
11. MY SON JEEP
12. Leopold Stokowski and his wife Gloria Vanderbilt, and Roy Campanella
13. Peter Sands/Don Porter
14. Cliff Robertson — ROD BROWN OF THE ROCKET RANGERS
15. THREE STEPS TO HEAVEN
16. ACTION IN THE AFTERNOON

17. THE BOB CROSBY SHOW
18. THE COMEBACK STORY
19. ETHEL AND ALBERT — Peg Lynch and Alan Bunce
20. Leon Ames and Lurene Tuttle
21. George Raft — I AM THE LAW
22. MEET THE VEEP — Alben W. Barkley
23. Ten years
24. YOU ARE THERE — Walter Cronkite

1954

1. Richard Webb, Ichabod Mudd/Sid Melton
2. DEAR PHOEBE — Bill Hastings/Peter Lawford
3. Roger Price
4. "Where the elite meet to eat"
5. THE DUKE
6. EARN YOUR VACATION — Johnny Carson
7. Jim Anderson . . . . Robert Young
   Margaret Anderson . . . . Jane Wyatt
   Betty Anderson (Princess) . . . . Elinor Donahue
   Kathy Anderson (Kitten) . . . . . Lauren Chapin
   Bud Anderson (Jim Jr.) . . . . . . Billy Grey
8. THE GREATEST GIFT
9. Celeste Anders — HONESTLY CELESTE
10. Mr. Raymond/Paul McGrath
11. Denny David and Steve Connors/Michael O'Shea and William Bishop
12. JANET DEAN REGISTERED NURSE — Ella Raines
13. Joe Kirkwood Jr.
14. Gary Merrill — JUSTICE
15. Warren Anderson, Tom Tully — THE LINEUP
16. THE MAIL STORY — HANDLE WITH CARE
17. MARRIOTT — Hume Cronyn and Jessica Tandy

18. Rocky Graziano
19. STORIES OF THE CENTURY
20. THAT'S MY BOY — Eddie Mayehoff
21. WATERFRONT — John Herrick, Cheryl Ann
22. June Havoc
23. Gene Rayburn
24. FACE THE NATION — George Herman and Stuart
    Novins

1955

1. Smilin Ed McConnell — SMILIN ED McCONNELL AND HIS GANG
   Andy Devine — ANDY'S GANG
2. BRAVE EAGLE — Keith Larson
3. CAPTAIN GALLANT OF THE FOREIGN LEGION or FOREIGN LEGIONNAIRE Buster Crabbe and Cullen Crabbe
4. CAPTAIN KANGAROO — Bob Keeshan
5. CASABLANCA — Charles McGraw
6. George Dolenz
7. CRUNCH AND DES — Crunch Adams and Des
8. THE CRUSADER — Brian Keith
9. Bobby Diamond
10. Summerfield — Willard Waterman
11. Janis Paige
12. JOE AND MABEL — Larry Blyden and Nita Talbot
13. Rosemary DeCamp and Dwayne Hickman
14. Tom Morrison
15. NORBY — David Wayne
16. PROFESSIONAL FATHER — Steve Dunne
17. Richard Greene
18. Truman Bradley

19. SECRET FILE U.S.A. — Robert Alda
20. Richard Simmons, King, Rex
21. SO THIS IS HOLLYWOOD — Mitzi Green and Virginia Gibson
22. A) Master Sergeant
    B) Company B, 24th Division
    C) Fremont
    D) Baxter
    E) Roseville, Kansas
23. Tuesday, eight thirty-nine P.M., Dodge City, Kansas, and Tombstone, Arizona
24. Marshal Matt Dillon and Dr. Galen (Doc) Adams

1956

1. James Cagney — ROBERT MONTGOMERY PRESENTS
2. Walter Cronkite
3. COMBAT SERGEANT
4. THE ADVENTURES OF HIRAM HOLIDAY — Wally Cox
5. JUDGE ROY BEAN — Edgar Buchanan
6. THE MAN CALLED X — Barry Sullivan
7. MY FRIEND FLICKA
8. Gale Storm
9. New Orleans Police Department — both played detectives
10. NOAH'S ARK — Paul Burke and Vic Rodman
11. THE GALE STORM SHOW (OH, SUSANNA) — Susanna Pomeroy, Miss Esmerelda (Nugey) Nugent
12. Rocky Lane
13. TALES OF THE 77TH BENGAL LANCERS — Warren Stevens, Philip Carey and Patrick Whyte
14. STANLEY — Carol Burnett
15. THE BROTHERS — Gale Gordon and Bob Sweeney
16. THE BUCCANEERS — Robert Shaw

17. THE ADVENTURES OF JIM BOWIE — Scott Forbes
18. NOTHING BUT THE TRUTH
19. THE ADVENTURES OF SIR LANCELOT — William Russell
20. Sonny Fox, Ralph Story
21. A) NBC B) Wednesday C) ten-thirty to eleven P.M.
22. WEST POINT — Donald May
23. Edgar Bergen
24. WIRE SERVICE — George Brent, Mercedes McCambridge and Dane Clark

1957

1. ASSIGNMENT FOREIGN LEGION
2. Pamela Britton and Arthur Lake
3. BOOTS AND SADDLES
4. THE COURT OF LAST RESORT
5. Liza Hammond — THE EVE ARDEN SHOW
6. ABC
7. THE GRAY GHOST — Major John Mosby
8. HARBOURMASTER — Barry Sullivan and Paul Burke
9. HAVE GUN WILL TRAVEL
10. June Cleaver (Mom) .... Barbara Billingsley
    Ward Cleaver (Dad) .... Hugh Beaumont
    Wally Cleaver (older son) ..... Tony Dow
    Theodore (The Beaver)
    Cleaver .... Jerry Mathers
11. M—SQUAD, Lieutenant Frank Ballinger/ Lee Marvin
12. MEET McGRAW — Frank Lovejoy
13. MR. ADAM AND EVE
14. Ron Randell — O.S.S.
15. Richard Crenna
16. John Payne — THE RESTLESS GUN

17. SALLY — Marion Lorne
18. Rod Cameron
19. TRACKDOWN — Robert Culp
20. THE TWENTIETH CENTURY — Walter Cronkite
21. TWENTY-SIX MEN
22. THE VERDICT IS YOURS
23. Jim Hardie
24. RICHARD DIAMOND, PRIVATE DETECTIVE

1958

1. A gold-tipped cane and derby hat
2. BUCKSKIN
3. Alan Hale Jr.
4. J. Carrol Naish and James Hong
5. CIMARRON CITY — George Montgomery
6. Stone, Hilldalle
7. Barbara Eden, Merry Anders, and Lori Nelson
8. THE INVESTIGATOR — Lonny Chapman and Howard St. John
9. Roger Moore
10. JEFFERSON DRUM
11. KALEIDOSCOPE
12. John Russell, Peter Brown — THE LAWMAN
13. LOVE THAT JILL — Barbara Nichols
14. Charles Bronson — MAN WITH A CAMERA
15. Darren McGavin
16. "There are eight million stories in the Naked City; this has been one of them."
17. NORTHWEST PASSAGE — Keith Larsen and Buddy Ebsen
18. Hope Emerson
19. RESCUE 8 — Jim Davis

20. Johnny Crawford
21. NBC — Dean Fredericks
22. THE TEXAN — Rory Calhoun
23. Jock Mahoney
24. CANNONBALL — Paul Birch and William Campbell

1959

1. Roger Moore, Jeff York, and Dorothy Provine
2. Elizabeth, Inger, and Marie
3. BOURBON STREET BEAT — Andrew Duggan and Richard Long
4. BRENNER — Edward Binns and James Broderick
5. Allen Ludden
6. Rod Cameron — CORONADO 9
7. Dennis O'Keefe — THE DENNIS O'KEEFE SHOW
8. Herbert Anderson and Gloria Henry
9. THE DEPUTY — Henry Fonda and Allen Case
10. Holbrook . . . . Robert Taylor
    Russo . . . . Tige Andrews
    Conway . . . . Lee Farr
    Lindstrom . . . . Russell Thorson
11. Frank Faylen and Florida Friebus
12. Bob Sweeney and Cathy Lewis
13. Roscoe Karns
14. Sundance/Earl Holliman
15. THE LAWLESS YEARS — James Gregory
16. LOVE AND MARRIAGE
17. George Nader — MAN AND THE CHALLENGE

18. THE MAN FROM BLACKHAWK — Robert Rockwell
19. Victor Jory and Patrick McVey
20. MEN INTO SPACE — William Lundigan
21. John Vivyan, Ross Martin
22. PECK'S BAD GIRL — Wendell Corey and Patty McCormack
23. JOHNNY STACCATO
24. THE TROUBLESHOOTERS — Keenan Wynn and Bob Mathias

THE 1950s PHOTO AND PROGRAM SCHEDULE ANSWERS

Photo Answers

1. Two years
2. Wally Cox, Tony Randall, Marion Lorne, Patricia Benoit
3. Eight years
4. Mr. & Mrs. Clarence Day Sr. (LIFE WITH FATHER)
5. Ronald Coleman — THE HALLS OF IVY
6. John Beresford Tipton — THE MILLIONAIRE
7. Longbranch Saloon — Russell
8. THE GALE STORM SHOW (OH, SUSANNA)
9. YOU'LL NEVER GET RICH
10. Hotel Carlton in San Francisco
11. Beaver's brother Wally
12. Steve Canyon, Mary Tyler Moore
13. THE DETECTIVES
14. BOURBON STREET BLUES
15. Mike Nelson — SEA HUNT

Program Schedule Answers

1. Bill Slater
2. Tony Marvin
3. Religious
4. Herb Shriner
5. Jan Murray
6. Dennis James
7. Bert Parks
8. Guy Williams
9. Win Elliot
10. Henry Mancini

The 1960s

QUESTIONS

1960

1. Johnny Carson, not known primarily as an actor, made one of his rare dramatic appearances playing opposite Anne Francis on this distinguished weekly television series. Name the series, and the particular drama Johnny Carson starred in.
2. THE AQUANAUTS was an hour-long adventure series about the experiences of two professional divers. However, by midseason the show's format along with a cast change resulted in a change of program title. What was the new name of this program?
3. Another sea adventure to debut in 1960 was ASSIGNMENT UNDERWATER. In this series a father and daughter teamed up to investigate and solve various criminal cases. Who starred in this show?
4. A young bachelor making his home with two spinster aunts was the theme of this situation comedy. Name the show and star.
5. CHECKMATE, Inc. was a sophisticated, well

equipped, and technically oriented private investigative agency. They not only solved crimes but helped to prevent them. Can you name the principal actors in this series?

6. A short-lived daytime soap opera with a different twist dramatized the problems faced by the first astronauts, their wives and families. What was the name of this serial?

7. Skip Homeier played a police lieutenant working out of the Hollywood Sheriff's office in this crime drama series. What was the name of the program?

8. What was the name of the first prime-time cartoon series made especially for television?

9. An urban and sophisticated New York couple dissatisfied with life in the big city bought a dude ranch in New Mexico, and then they *really* had problems. Bill and Babs Hooten were the principal characters in this situation comedy series. Name the show and the stars.

10. A father and son team of attorneys: the father hardened by many years of experience, and the son fresh out of law school. Their contrasting styles made this situation comedy interesting. Can you name the show and the stars?

11. Glenn Evans was an American journalist living and working in Hong Kong in this adventure series. Who played Glenn Evans and what was the name of the show?

12. A tropical setting in the Spice Islands was the background for this hour-long adventure series about two men who owned a one-plane airline service. Can you name this program?

13. This was another adventure series set in Alaska during the Gold Rush of the 1890s. By midseason the program was cancelled and one of the actors went on to eventually become a very famous film star. Name the actor and the series.

14. An attorney with the name Abraham Lincoln Jones had to be as honest and forthright as humanly

possible. This was the name of the main character in the series THE LAW AND MR. JONES. Who played the lead role?

15. A one-season international crime drama starred Richard Wyler as Anthony Smith, special agent. What was the name of this series?

16. A book, several plays and movies preceded this comedy series about two sisters, one a writer, and one an aspiring actress, trying to further their careers. Name the program and who played the sisters.

17. Fred MacMurray starred as Steve Douglas, a widower, during the long-running situation comedy MY THREE SONS. Who played Fred MacMurray's first three sons and what were their character names?

18. The Brown family owned a farm, and young Velvet Brown was trying to train her horse to compete in the Grand National Steeplechase in this drama. What was the name of the program and who played Velvet Brown?

19. The Overland Stage Company provided the first coach line to run from Missouri to California and back. This was the setting for an hour-long western series starring William Bendix. Name the series and the other star.

20. PETE AND GLADYS was a half-hour comedy series and a spinoff from DECEMBER BRIDE, about an insurance salesman and his silly wife. Who played Pete and Gladys?

21. Set in New York City, two investigative reporters and a singer made up a trio who were exposing many of the rackets and gangsters that were controlling the city during prohibition. What was the name of this program and who were the stars?

22. Can you remember the names of the two guys who traveled on ROUTE 66 in their 1960 Corvette and who played them?

23. David McLean starred as a one-armed gunfighter who battled injustice in this western series. Name the program.

117

24. Paul Morgan was a fun-loving bachelor who made his living as a cartoonist in this comedy series. Who played Paul Morgan and what was the name of the show?

1961

1. ABC's durable Saturday afternoon sports anthology WIDE WORLD OF SPORTS has covered every known type of competitive event throughout the world. Who is the host that has been with the program since the beginning and what was the date of the first telecast?

2. THE FLINTSTONES and BUGS BUNNY had already become popular prime-time cartoon shows when this animated series was introduced to evening audiences. What was the name of the program and on what network did it debut?

3. The Canfield brothers were Virginian farmers who fought on opposite sides during the Civil War. Can you name this Civil War drama series?

4. This police series, based on a 1950 film, was about the investigations of a specialist group of detectives who infiltrated the inner circle of the underworld. Matt Gower and Gus Honochek were the principal characters. Name the show and the stars.

5. Dr. David Zorba was Chief of Neurosurgery, and Dr. Ben Casey's boss and friend on this popular medical series BEN CASEY. Upon Dr. Zorba's departure who became the new Chief and what actor portrayed this role?

6. The Sherwood Diner in Sunrise, Colorado was the

background setting for this dramatic series about the people passing through the town. Name the show and the star.

7. A gangland lawyer decided to reform and become an agent of the Federal Government to help in the fight against the warlords of crime. What was the name of this crime drama and who was the star?

8. A situation comedy about police officers was titled CAR 54, WHERE ARE YOU? Can you name the principal characters and who played them?

9. John Drake was a special investigator for the North Atlantic Treaty Organization (NATO) in this international intrigue series produced in England. What was the name of the series and who was the star?

10. This was a well-written courtroom drama series which revolved around a father and son team of trial lawyers. The program was titled ＿＿＿ ＿＿＿＿＿, ran for four years on the CBS network and starred ＿＿ ＿＿ ＿＿＿＿＿ and ＿＿＿ ＿＿＿.

11. Dick Van Dyke played head comedy writer, Rob Petrie on THE DICK VAN DYKE SHOW. What was the name of the show he wrote for?

12. DR. KILDARE, like BEN CASEY, was a very popular medical show which enjoyed a five-year run on television. Can you name the senior doctor Kildare worked with and the name of the hospital that employed them?

13. Steve Carella was one of the police detectives who worked out of Manhattan's 87th Precinct. This was a standard police drama, but Carella's wife had a physical handicap which made the program a little different. Who played Steve Carella, what was his wife's handicap and who played her?

14. Leon Ames, who years before played the father in LIFE WITH FATHER now played a similar role in FATHER OF THE BRIDE. What was the family name and where did they live?

15. The Thompson and Travis Circus traveled from town to town in a wagon train which provided the background for this hour-long western drama. Casey

Thompson, played by _____ _____, and Ben Travis, played by _____ _____, were the stars of this series titled _____ _____.

16. One of the last live dramatic shows on television was hosted by Frank Gallop. Among the actors who appeared in this series were Robert Duvall, Arthur Hill, Lee Grant, and Richard Thomas. Name the program.

17. Tony Young played Cord, an undercover agent of the U.S. Cavalry. His commanding officer was Captain Zachary Wingate. What was the name of this western program and who played the commanding officer?

18. THE HATHAWAYS were a family of five in this situation comedy. However, only two were humans, the other three were chimps. Who played the humans?

19. HAZEL was a popular comic strip which came to life on television and starred Shirley Booth. What was Hazel's full name, and what was the name of the family she worked for?

20. MR. ED was a half-hour comedy series about an unusual horse. Alan Young played Wilbur Post, an architect who discovered that he owned a talking horse. Who was the voice of Mr. Ed?

21. As unlikely as it may seem, this comedy series was about a pair of newlyweds living with the wife's parents and grandparents. In other words, three generations of families living under one roof. Can you name the program and who played the newlyweds?

22. Walter Matthau made many guest appearances on television in the 1950s and 1960s. However, he only starred in one weekly series. _____ _____ was a crime drama and he played the role of Lex Rogers, special agent.

23. Paul Marino was an investigative reporter on _____ ____ _____, an hour long newspaper drama show, starring _____ _____.

24. Insurance investigator _____ _____ played by George Nader was the principal character in _____.

1962

1. Sergeant Chip Sanders and Lieutenant Gil Hanley, played by _____ _____ and _____ _____, led their platoon across Europe following D-Day in the World War II drama _____ on the __ __ __ network.
2. Not all military series were serious or set in wartime. ENSIGN O'TOOLE was just that type of program. This was a military comedy about a destroyer vessel in peacetime in the South Pacific. Who played Ensign O'Toole and what was the name of the destroyer?
3. FAIR EXCHANGE was originally developed as an hour-long situation comedy. It was the story of an American family and a British family who exchanged their teenage daughters, Patty Walker and Heather Finch, for a year. Can you remember who played these characters?
4. Two carpenters were the central characters in this sitcom starring John Astin and Marty Ingels. Name the program and the characters they played.
5. McHALE'S NAVY was one of the most popular of all comedy series and paralleled the Sergeant Bilko program of prior years. Originally the program was set in one area of the globe and then another. Can you name the two areas?
6. A political comedy series, based on an earlier motion

picture, was about a rural politican who becomes a senator and goes off to the struggles and frustrations of adjusting to life in the nation's capital. What was the name of the series and star?

7. Christine Massey was a widow with seven children living in the suburbs and made her living as a magazine writer. Who played Christine and what was the name of this comedy-drama series?

8. THE NURSES was an hour-long medical drama about the personal and professional lives of two nurses working in a large city hospital. The characters were Nurse Liz Thorpe and Nurse Gail Lucas. Who were the stars?

9. Stanley Holloway from "My Fair Lady" fame was the star of this comedy series about an English butler who was inherited by an American middle-class family. What was the name of the series?

10. An adventure series about two sky-diving instructors was titled RIPCORD. One of the stars would go on to become famous as a character in the popular western series GUNSMOKE. Who was that star?

11. ROOM FOR ONE MORE was a situation comedy based on a 1952 film starring Cary Grant and Betsy Drake as parents of four children. Who played the TV parents?

12. Nick Adams and John Larkin played crusading newspaper people in this hour-long series on NBC. What was the name of the program?

13. Edmond O'Brien played ____ _____ in this hour-long show of the same name, which was based on the real-life trial lawyer Jacob W. "Jake" Erlich.

14. This western series was about a champion rodeo rider, Stoney Burke, played by ____ _____. He was always seeking ____ ____ _____, the trophy that is awarded to the world's best bronco rider.

15. Television's first ninety-minute western, _____ _____ ran for many years and only two of the cast members, _____ _____ and _____ _____ remained with the program for its entire run.

16. Another western series set along the professional rodeo circuit premiered in 1962 and was about two brothers and their experiences. What was the name of the program and who were the stars?

17. ABC's other World War II drama GALLANT MEN did not have the success that COMBAT did and was off the air after one season. Can you name the two principal characters and who played them in this wartime drama?

18. Douglas "Mr. Pocus" Anderson, Phil "Coo Coo" Kiley, Bonnie Lee and Ringmaster Claude Kirchner were all regulars on what Saturday morning show?

19. MAN OF THE WORLD was a mystery series about an American journalist and his assignments throughout the world. Who was the star of this show?

20. Terrence Morgan played _____ _____ _____, commander of The Golden Hind, in this adventure series set in sixteenth-century England.

21. John Lackland, a successful businessman, decides to forsake his career and retreat to a South Pacific island for the tranquility it offers. What is the name of this series and who was the star?

22. Father O'Malley and his superior Father Fitzgibbon were the parish priests in a run-down New York City neighborhood in this comedy/drama series based on a popular motion picture. Name the series and the stars.

23. What program did Groucho Marx host after the conclusion of the original YOU BET YOUR LIFE series?

24. A popular daytime game show which featured a celebrity panel trying to guess the identity of mystery guests from clues given by Host Dennis James was titled _____ _____ _____.

1963

1. ARREST AND TRIAL was an unusual ninety-minute crime drama. The first half depicted the committing of the crime, and the police making an arrest. The second half concerned the trial of the defendants. Who played the principal role in the arrest segment, and who played the leading role in the trial?
2. Author/correspondent Jim Bishop narrated a World War II weekly documentary series titled _____ _____.
3. Paul Richards and Edward Franz played the roles of psychiatrists in a large metropolitan hospital in this weekly series. Can you name this medical drama, and the hospital in which the stories took place?
4. Danny Kaye, a most versatile performer, began hosting his own musical/variety/comedy show in 1963. On what network was the show and for how many years did it run?
5. A well-done dramatic series about social workers and how they deal with the many problems of the aged, drug addiction, race relations, the poor, etc., was titled ____ ____ ____ _____, and starred _____ __ _____.
6. Katy Holstrom was a young woman from Minnesota who came to the nation's capital and got a job as

housekeeper for Congressman Glen Morley in this comedy series. What was the name of the show and who were the stars?

7. Television's all-time popular chase series THE FUGITIVE starred David Janssen as Dr. Richard Kimble, the accussed killer of his wife Helen. Who played his wife in the flashback scenes?

8. Johnny Slate was the working boss and Otto King the business manager of this circus drama series based on a 1950s film. What was the name of the series and who were the stars?

9. GRINDL was a household domestic who worked for the Foster Temporary Domestic Employment Agency in this half-hour comedy series. Who played Grindl?

10. What was the name of the Saturday morning NBC cartoon series about a scientist, who was assisted by a mouse and an elephant, and had a time machine?

11. James Franciscus played an English teacher, John Novak, in the drama series MR. NOVAK. Dean Jagger was the principal at the school where Novak taught. Can you name the school and the principal's name?

12. Phil Silvers was up to his old tricks again trying to hustle anybody and everybody in his new series, THE NEW PHIL SILVERS SHOW. What was the name of the character he played and what was his occupation?

13. An hour-long western starring Jeffrey Hunter was about a traveling circuit-court attorney who was adept with a gun as well as his words. Name the character and the program.

14. Bill Dana played _____, a bellhop at a New York hotel in __ ____ ____ ____ .

15. In this series a millionaire police chief would arrive at the scene of a crime in a luxurious automobile.
    A) What was the name of this show?
    B) Can you name the police chief?
    C) What was the make of the car?
    D) Who played the role?

16. CASPER THE FRIENDLY GHOST was a very popular Saturday morning program for youngsters during the 1960s. What network was it on?

17. A well-done documentary series about the motion picture industry was titled HOLLYWOOD AND THE STARS. Who was the host and narrator?

18. HOOTENANNY was a traveling folk musical festival taped at a different college campus each week. Who was the host of this show?

19. Two very popular daytime serials began on the same day and still remain popular after all these years. Name the serials and their respective networks, and the day they commenced.

20. The longest-running documentary series about animal life premiered on Sunday afternoon, January 6, 1963. What was the name of this series and what network was it originally seen?

21. Gene Roddenberry, future creator of STAR TREK, produced this hour-long dramatic series about an officer's life in the peacetime Marine Corp. What was the name of the series and who were the stars?

22. MISSING LINKS was a game show that was originally hosted by _____ _____ on NBC, and then hosted by _____ _____ on ABC.

23. Long before MEDICAL CENTER, Chad Everett played a deputy in a western series. Can you name the series?

24. WORD FOR WORD was a daytime game show that was hosted by what famous talk-show host?

1964

1. What was the name of the charter boat on GILLI-GAN'S ISLAND which was caught in a storm and left the passengers stranded on an unchartered South Pacific isle?
2. Paul Ford played a crusty old sea captain of a charter fishing boat in this comedy series, which also starred Stanley Holloway and Judy Carne. What was the name of this show?
3. New Caledonia in the South Pacific was the setting for this military comedy series about four U.S. Navy Waves. Essentially this was another McHALE'S NAVY. What was the name of this comedy series?
4. Fess Parker played one of America's favorite folk heroes, DANIEL BOONE, in a series of the same name, which had a long run on the NBC network. What was the name of Daniel Boone's college-educated Indian friend and who played him?
5. Napoleon Solo and Illya Kuryakin were the two fearless agents who worked for U.N.C.L.E., the international crime-fighting organization. What does the acronym UNCLE stand for?
6. Walter Burnley was the manager of the complaint department in Krockmeyer's Department Store.

What comedy does this character come from and who portrayed the role?

7. Mike Bell, a public relations man, was the principal character in this short-lived but interesting drama series about important people's desire to have a good public image. What was the name of the series and who was the star?

8. THE MUNSTERS were a strange family indeed. The only normal member was the Munster's niece, Marilyn, played originally by _____ _____ and then by _____ _____.

9. THE ROGUES was a light drama about a family of charming con artists. What stars made up this family?

10. Richard Crenna played an idealistic politician in this dramatic series which lasted only a little more than a season on CBS. What was the name of this drama series?

11. VOYAGE TO THE BOTTOM OF THE SEA was an hour-long science fiction series set aboard the American research submarine Seaview. You probably remember Richard Basehart as Admiral Harriman Nelson, but who played Captain Lee Crane, and try this one: who played Lieutenant Commander Chip Morton?

12. THE ADDAMS FAMILY were not your typical family you would like as your next-door neighbors, but they were fun to watch on TV. What were the names of the children and who played them?

13. Fenwick Diversified Industries did not permit married couples to work for the company. Cara and Frank Bridges were secretly married and employed at Fenwick. This of course made for many comical experiences in their daily working lives. Who played Cara and Frank and what was the name of the show?

14. Everybody remembers FLIPPER the dolphin who was a friend and helper to Porter Ricks, the chief ranger at Coral Key Park, Florida, in this adventure show of the same name. Can you name the actor who played Porter Ricks?

15. The HOLLYWOOD PALACE was a big-budgeted all-star variety show that was on the ABC network for six years. Each week a different celebrity hosted the show. However, one host in particular was associated with the show because of his many appearances. Who was he?

16. Shortly after Dennis Weaver left the GUNSMOKE series he starred in his own comedy/drama series. What was the name of this series and who was the character he played?

17. What personality did ABC employ in their first attempt at a late night talk show to compete with Johnny Carson?

18. Mickey Grady inherited a run down seaside hotel and then his problems began. This made for many comical episodes about management/ownership of a vacation resort. The series' star also had one of his own children featured as a permanent member of the cast. Who was the star, what was his son's name, and can you name the series?

19. MR. MAGOO, that cantankerous, bumbling, near-sighted old man, starred in many theatrical cartoons, had his own prime-time series for one season. Who was the voice of Mr. Magoo?

20. Julie Newmar was Rhoda, a government secret project in this situation comedy series. Why was Rhoda considered a government project, and what was the name of this series?

21. NO TIME FOR SERGEANTS was a military comedy series which had success as a Broadway show and then a movie with Andy Griffith starring in both, before becoming a weekly television program. What was the name of the central character, who played the role, and in what branch of the service was the story set?

22. When it was in its heydey, PEYTON PLACE was television's only successful prime-time soap opera. Initially it ran two nights a week, and then three. Can you remember on what network PEYTON PLACE

was televised and on which two nights of the week it originally ran?

23. President John F. Kennedy had written a book when he was a Senator about American political figures who faced difficult decisions during their careers. His book eventually became a documentary television series. What was the name of this series?

24. Valentine Farrow was a playboy publishing executive in New York who had a glamorous lifestyle in this comedy series. Who played Valentine Farrow and what was the name of the show?

1965

1. An inane weekly series about two summer camps for children had the appropriate program title of _____ _____.

2. Generally, wartime drama programs lasted at least one television season. This series, about the U.S. Navy, only ran for thirteen weeks, and starred John Gavin and John Larch. What was the name of this short-lived series?

3. F TROOP was made up of a crew of bumblers and incompetents who were led by a commanding officer without the experience of command. Who was this "leader" and what actor portrayed the role?

4. Artistically acclaimed, but low in the ratings, this police drama series starred William Shatner as an assistant district attorney whose zeal for justice brought him more trouble then he could handle. What was the name of this series?

5. Agents 86 and 99, played by Don Adams and Barbara Feldon, worked for _____, the U.S. Intelligence Agency which was constantly trying to defeat the diabolical plots of _____, the organization of evil.

6. Francis Lawrence was the formal name of a fifteen-and-a-half-year-old teenager in this situation comedy

titled after her more common name. What was the name of the series and who played her?

7. One of TV's earliest female private eyes had many of James Bond skills and gimmickry and was really a sexy-looking sleuth. What was her name, and who played her?

8. Kelly Robinson and Alexander Scott were undercover agents played by ____ ____ and ____ ____ on the popular spy program ____ ____.

9. The Robinson family was scheduled to take a five-year voyage to the Alphi Centauri star system, but due to some malfunctions were thrown off-course. This was the setting for the popular space program LOST IN SPACE. Who played John and Maureen Robinson?

10. A MAN CALLED SHENANDOAH was about a man without a memory wandering the west trying to find out who he was and where he belonged. Who starred in this role?

11. This situation comedy was about an actress who made lots of money, played by Juliet Prowse, and is married to a U.S. Air Force sergeant. Not to make him feel inferior they try to live on his meager salary of $500 a month. What was the name of this series?

12. THE NURSES was a prime-time medical series which was popular for three years and then became a daytime serial. In the soap opera version, the principal characters, Nurses Liz Thorpe and Gail Lucas remained the same but were played by different actresses. Can you name them?

13. O.K. Crackerby was a widower, somewhat rough and crude and lacked the social graces to be accepted into the world of high society. However, he also happened to be the world's richest man. Who played this role in this comedy series?

14. Dennis James hosted a popular game show titled P.D.Q. What does P.D.Q. stand for?

15. PLEASE DON'T EAT THE DAISIES was the story about a suburban wife and mother, who was also a freelance writer, her college professor/husband and

their four children. Who starred as the parents in this family comedy series?

16. Ben Gazzara played the role of ____ _____ a lawyer on _____, which was a story of a man who had less than two years to live.

17. Peter Falk played a talented and brilliant New York defense attorney in this hour-long drama series. However, this character led a very disorganized personal lifestyle which made for many comical moments each week on this program. What was the name of the program?

18. Major Simon Butcher and Lieutenant Richard "Rip" Riddle were the senior officers aboard the USS _____ in the war adventure series ____ _____ ____ __ __ _____ starring ____ _____ and ____ _____.

19. Robert Conrad and Ross Martin were the government undercover agents in this popular western series THE WILD WILD WEST. Their job was such that they reported directly to the President of The United States. Who was that President?

20. NBC already had the Cartwrights in the BONANZA series, so ABC introduced the Barkley family living on a big sprawling ranch in California. Name this western series and who played the head of the family.

21. Dean Martin began hosting his own hour-long variety show in 1965 on the NBC network. How many seasons did his show last?

22. For many years THE F.B.I. was seen on _____ night at _____ o'clock on the __ __ __ network.

23. Hooterville was the setting for this successful rural situation comedy series which featured Pat Buttram and Tom Lester. Name the series, the stars, and the characters they played.

24. Several months after ABC had introduced the first prime-time quality rock-and-roll series, one of the other networks introduced their own. Can you name the show and network?

1966

1. A spy comedy series about a mild-mannered accountant employed by Central Intelligence was titled __ ___ ___ __ ____ ____ and starred ____ _____.

2. Jack Whitaker, now a CBS sports reporter, hosted a prime-time Saturday night game show in which contestants had to identify famous personalities from cut-up sections of a facial photograph. What was the name of the show?

3. THE GIRL FROM U.N.C.L.E. was a spinoff from THE MAN FROM U.N.C.L.E., but had far less success. Who was the star and what was the name of the character she portrayed?

4. A very popular crime fighter who was a radio audience favorite during the 1930s and 1940s came to television in 1966. Can you name the crime fighter and who played the role?

5. The Buffalo Pass and Scalplock Railroad was only half completed and near bankruptcy when Ben Calhoun won it in a poker game. This takes place in the first episode, and then the story line concerns itself with problems of completing the railroad. Name the series and the star.

6. Don Francks, John Leyton, and Marino Mase starred in this World War II adventure series about three

allied agents working behind enemy lines. What was the name of this series?

7. David and Julie Willis were a young married couple living in San Francisco trying to make ends meet in this situation comedy series. Can you name the series and the stars?

8. THE MONKEES were a rock-and-roll group who were always getting themselves into some escapade in this weekly thirty-minute comedy series. What were the names of The Monkees?

9. Wretched, Colorado was the setting for this western comedy series about the Hanks family. Three generations of them, trying to help maintain law and order in their town. What famous motion picture actress played the lead and can you name this western series?

10. ____ _____ played the lead in a sitcom about a wealthy Long Island family who went from riches to rags, and how they managed to stay afloat in this series titled __ _____ __ _____.

11. One of the more popular adventure series was about a squad of four men traveling in two jeeps, fighting Germans in the North African desert. What was the name of this series and who was the star?

12. The classic motion picture SHANE became a short-lived hour-long western series starring _____ _____.

13. T.H.E. CAT was an adventure series about a former circus aerialist turned cat-burglar who then turned to fighting crime. What does T.H.E. Cat stand for?

14. You probably recall that Marlo Thomas played Ann Marie, a young actress looking for her big break in New York. Like many other artistic people she lived on Manhattan's upper west side. Do you know where Ann Marie grew up?

15. Dr. Tony Newman and Dr. Doug Phillips were two scientists who developed a machine that transported people into the past or future in the hour-long science fiction series __ ____ _____, starring ____ ____ and ____ _____.

16. David March posed as a foreign correspondent but was actually an American double agent who had infiltrated the German intelligence service in this spy drama series. What was the name of the series and who played David March?

17. Another police drama series which took place in Los Angeles had father and son assigned to the same precinct. Son Jim Briggs was a detective and father Dan Briggs was the desk sergeant. Name the series and who played these characters.

18. Sam Garrett was a clumsy, awkward, two-left-feet type of person in his everyday life. On screen he portrayed a cool and fearless character, "Jed Clayton, U.S. Marshall." The title of this series about a popular TV star was ____ ____ and starred _____ _____.

19. This space age comedy series was about two astronauts on a NASA mission and somehow encounter a mechanical problem which moves their spacecraft back in time to a prehistoric age. They befriend a stone-age family and try to adjust to life in this era. What was the name of this comedy series and who played the astronauts?

20. Michael Callan and Patricia Harty played the lead roles in this situation comedy series about a company who only hired married men. Can you name this comedy series?

21. Tammy Ward was an heiress who is restricted to a tight budget by her stingy uncle in this comedy series which ran for only four episodes. Name this very short-run series.

22. Batman, the famous comic book hero, generated much interest during its two-year run in prime-time television. One of its most appealing features was the use of famous personalities as villains. See if you can name the stars who played these wicked rogues.
   A) The Joker .... _____ _____
   B) The Penguin .... _____ _____
   C) The Riddler .... _____ _____
   D) The Archer .... _____ _____

E) The Black Widow..... ———————— ————————
F) Egghead .... ———————— ————————
G) The Minstrel .... ———————— ————————
H) The Bookworm....... ———————— ————————
I) King Tut............. ———————— ————————
J) The Sandman .... ———————— ————————

23. The syndicate was after Buddy Overstreet, a "Mr. Average Nice Guy," because of what he overheard in the comedy series ——— ——— ——— starring Jack ————————.

24. WAYNE AND SHUSTER TAKE AN AFFECTIONATE LOOK AT . . . was a long title for a very short-run program. What type of a program was it?

1967

1. Here was another comedy series about a widowed parent having to raise a child. This time the parent was a Las Vegas nightclub comic. Name the program and star.
2. AWAY WE GO was the title of a summer replacement program for the Jackie Gleason show. What comedian was one of the regular hosts?
3. Carter Nash was a ____ _____ who devised a potion that would transform him into ____ _____, crime fighter. _____ _____ was the star of this comedy series.
4. CBS made a decision to air television's third ninety-minute western, anticipating it would achieve the same success as the first two. Can you name this western series?
5. Jim Sinclair was a world champion rodeo rider who goes to Kenya to help set up modern ranching methods in this adventure series. What was the name of this series and who was the star?
6. In the short-lived series THE LEGEND OF CUSTER, who played the famous American military figure?
7. DUNDEE AND THE CULHANE was the story of an experienced British lawyer and his assistant, an American lawyer, who travel throughout the west in

the interest of justice. What actors starred in this law-and-order western series?

8. You probably remember that Sister Bertrille was the effervescent novice nun who discovered she could fly in the comedy series THE FLYING NUN, but what was her former name?

9. Four convicts made up this special squad who were trained to fight behind enemy lines during World War II. If they survived the war they would be granted a presidential pardon. What was the name of this war drama series?

10. Dave Lewis and Larry Clarke co-hosted an early-morning radio show in the situation comedy series ___ ____ _____. Ronnie Schell played one of the disc jockeys and _____ _____ the other.

11. _____ _____ and _____ _____, married to each other in real life, played a cartoonist and his wife, in the comedy series ___ ___ _____.

12. THE HIGH CHAPARRAL was a successful western series, running for several years on NBC. What were the names of the two principal families in this series?

13. Joey Bishop competed with Johnny Carson for two-and-a-half years in the battle for late-night viewers. Who was his sidekick on the show?

14. Carl Betz played a high powered, expensive attorney, Clinton Judd on _____ _____ _____ _____.

15. What was the name of the daytime serial that was based on a mid-50s film of the same name?

16. _____ _____ played Stanley Beamish, gas station proprietor, who took power pills to become ___ _____, the caped fighter of crime and injustice.

17. The Hubbards and The Buells were neighbors whose children were married to each other in this suburban family comedy series. What was the name of this show?

18. Stories related to the Texas Rangers were generally depicted in a serious manner. This particular series was a comic western about an inept ranger. Can you name this series and its star?

19. Luke Carpenter was a gold prospector in Alaska at

the turn of the century and was lost in a glacier avalanche. Many years later he turned up, not having aged physically or mentally. This was the background for what situation comedy and who played this role?

20. SNAP JUDGEMENT was a daytime word game show originally hosted by ____ _____ on the ____ network.

21. A Saturday morning popular cartoon series was Marvel Comics' SPIDERMAN on the ABC network. Do you know Spiderman's identity?

22. In 1967 THE CAROL BURNET SHOW began on CBS. For how many years was it a network show?

23. Hondo Lane was an Army scout, troubleshooter, and special agent who was always trying to solve the problems between the white men and the Indians in the Arizona territory. Who played the title role in HONDO?

24. Long before FAMILY FEUD, there was another game show in which families competed. Can you name the show and host?

1968

1. More than a decade earlier, the first attempt to successfully bring BLONDIE, the comic strip, to television failed. A second try took place in 1968 and met with similar results. Who played Blondie and Dagwood Bumstead in this series?
2. THE CHAMPIONS were three undercover agents with special powers who worked for a Swiss-based international crime-fighting agency. Who were the stars of this adventure series?
3. What was the name of the ghost and what actor played the role on THE GHOST AND MRS. MUIR?
4. Two life-long friends pool their resources and buy a diner in this comedy series which ran for a short time on CBS. Name the series and stars.
5. Will Sonnett was a former cavalry scout who raised his grandson. Together they traveled the west to find the boy's father. What was the name of this western series and who were the stars?
6. Robert Wagner starred as Alexander Mundy, a professional thief who had style, in this adventure series IT TAKES A THIEF. He was recruited by a government agency under the direction of _____ _____, played by _____ _____, co-star of the series.

7. LANCER was an hour-long western set in California in the 1870s about a man and his sons running a very large cattle and lumber ranch. Who were the stars?

8. Captain Adam Greer was the head of THE MOD SQUAD. Can you name the others who made up this special unit and who portrayed these roles?

9. THE NAME OF THE GAME was a ninety-minute program which was actually three series in one. Who were the three principal characters, what were their occupations, and who played them?

10. Two bounty hunters, a Virginian aristocrat who lost everything in the war, and a freed slave, teamed up in an effort to make money by tracking down criminals in this western series. What was the name of this western series and who were the stars?

11. David Ross was an ex-con, pardoned for a crime he did not commit, who became a private detective. Can you name this crime series and the star?

12. This was an interesting prime-time summer replacement show which aired a number of different dramas that did not become weekly series. Name the program.

13. JULIA was a situation comedy about a widow trying to raise her son. A) What was Julia's full name and who played her? B) What was her son's name and who played him?

14. John McGill was a private detective, based in London, who was always available to fight crime anywhere in the world. Name this detective series and who was the star?

15. MAYBERRY R.F.D. succeeded THE ANDY GRIFFITH SHOW and starred _____ _____ as _____ _____, farmer and town councilor, and _____ _____ who played the role of his son _____.

16. The ABC Network presented a weekly variety show staged at a different military location each week. What was the name of this program?

17. An outstanding mystery adventure series in which the characters were identified by numbers was titled _____ _____ and starred _____ _____.

143

18. 60 MINUTES began in 1968 and was co-hosted by ____ _____ and ____ _____.

19. Tim Blair, talent agent, and Timmie Blair, model were one and the same, played by ____ _____ in the comedy series ____ ____ ____ ____ _____.

20. Martin Milner and Kent McCord shared a Los Angeles Police Department patrol car for seven television seasons on ADAM-12. What was the name of the characters they portrayed?

21. There was a short-lived daytime game show titled THE BABY GAME on which husband and wife teams tested their knowledge about babies. The host became known as "America's favorite baby-sitter". Who was he?

22. For a short time Phyllis Diller hosted her own variety show. What was the title of the program?

23. DREAM HOUSE was both a daytime and nighttime game show this year and gave contestants an opportunity to win a dream house worth up to $40,000. Who hosted both shows?

24. What was the name of the program that was the summer replacement for THE DEAN MARTIN SHOW for several years?

1969

1. During the first season of BRACKEN'S WORLD, John Bracken, the head of the studio, was not seen. He was revealed in the second season. Who played John Bracken?
2. The Corbetts, Tom the father and Eddie the son, were also best friends in this comedy series about a motherless household. Name the program and the actors who portrayed the father and the son.
3. THE GOVERNOR AND J.J. starred _____ as Governor William Drinkwater and ___ _____ as his daughter.
4. Two very popular medical drama series began in 1969 and were to last for seven years. Name them.
5. John Monroe was a writer and cartoonist who worked for Manhattanite Magazine in this comedy series on NBC. Who played John Monroe and what was the name of this weekly show?
6. Pete Dixon was a black American history teacher whose classes were held in ROOM 222 at a Los Angeles high school. Who played Pete Dixon and what was the name of the high school on this weekly series?
7. A very expensive hour-long dramatic series about the very rich and powerful starred one of Hollywood's

most famous actresses, making her television debut. Name the program and this actress.

8. Jim Bronson resigned his job and began to travel across the country on his motorcycle in the adventure series ___ ___ ___, starring ___ ___.

9. Chet Kincaid was a physical education teacher at Richard Allen Holmes High School and just an all-around good guy in this comedy series. Who played Chet Kincaid and what was the name of the program?

10. In his only continuing television role, movie star Dana Andrews played the president of a small midwestern college in a soap opera which ran on NBC for three-and-one-half years. Name this show.

11. Longfellow Deeds was a young midwestern newspaperman, played by ___ ___, who inherited a multimillion-dollar enterprise from a relative in the comedy series ___ ___ ___ ___ ___.

12. John Woodruff and Tony Novello made a fine private investigation team in this short-lived sixty-minute crime show. What was the name of the program and who were the stars?

13. On Monday nights, ABC presented two forty-five minute programs back to back. What were the names of the two programs?

14. Charles Duffy, Oliver Nelson and Seaman Becker were three of the comical crew members in this weekly series about an aging ocean liner. Name the program and the ocean liner?

15. What Saturday morning cartoon show featured a cowardly great dane, and four teenagers, Freddy, Daphne, Shaggy, and Velma?

16. Tim Conway had the unpleasant distinction of being involved in a comedy/variety series which was one of television's biggest flops. What was the name of the program and how long did it last?

17. THE BOLD ONES was an overall title under which four different drama series flourished. Can you name each of the series?

18. On Saturday mornings, what was the name of the

cartoon series about World War I fighting aviators and their escapades?

19. A popular film star played the role of a housewife who wanted to be a newspaper feature writer in a comedy series named after her. Who was she?

20. What was the name of the cartoon series about a simple-minded and naïve Royal Canadian Mounted Policeman?

21. A short-lived prime-time quiz show composed of a team of three teenagers and a team of three adults asking each other questions about their lifestyle was entitled _____ _____ _____.

22. With the public's interest in news and information increasing, NBC developed a two-hour news magazine program. Name the show and the original host.

23. THE GALLOPING GOURMET was a popular food preparation show sprinkled with humor. Who was the cullinary expert who hosted the show?

24. What former professional football star began hosting his own talk/variety show?

Photo Album

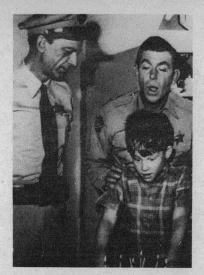

Question 1:
Who is the little boy making a birthday wish, and in what town and state did he live?

Question 2:
This pensive-looking team was always getting into comical situations inside and outside their station house. What precinct were they assigned to?

149

Question 3:
There were always laughs in this home because he was a comedy writer, but who were their nice but often befuddled next-door neighbors?

Question 4:
The Clampetts were suspicious of everybody throughout their long-running comedy series. On what night of the week did they appear for most of that time?

Question 5:
Of all the World War II action series this enjoyed the longest tenure. Name the program and how many years it ran.

Question 6:
Who are the two actors on the left waiting for an answer from Ben Gazzara and what was the name of the program?

Question 7:
For seven years this comedy series was a favorite with television viewers. What was the family's name and in what town did they live?

Question 8:
This bizarre family was fun to watch on television, but you probably would not have wanted them as your neighbors. What was their address?

Question 9:
Throughout this series, who was always chasing this man?

Question 10:
Agents 86 and 99 worked for "The Chief." What actor played that role?

Question 11:
Brian Keith starred in this show for five years.
Name the program and the character he played.

Question 12:
The IMF could accomplish just about anything.
Who was the original leader?

Question 13:
This man once had his own syndicated talk show. Who is he?

Question 14:
Steve McGarrett, Five-0's fearless leader, was directly responsible to the governor of Hawaii. Who played the role of the governor?

Question 15:
Who is missing from this picture?

Prime-Time
Network Program
Schedules

		7PM	7:30	8PM	8:30
Sunday	ABC	Walt Disney Presents		Maverick	The Lawman
	CBS	Lassie	Dennis The Menace	The Ed Sullivan Show	
	NBC	Shirley Temple's Storybook		National Velvet	Tab Hunter Show
Monday	ABC			Cheyenne	Surfside Six
	CBS		To Tell The Truth	Pete & Gladys	Bringing Up Buddy
	NBC			River Boat	Tales of Wells Fargo
Tuesday	ABC		Bugs Bunny Show	The Rifleman	Wyatt Earp
	CBS			Father Knows Best	Dobie Gillis
	NBC			Laramie	Alfred Hitchcock
Wednesday	ABC			Hong Kong	Ozzie and Harriet
	CBS			The Aquanauts	Wanted: Dead or Alive
	NBC			Wagon Train	Price Is Right
Thursday	ABC		Guestward Ho	Donna Reed Show	Real McCoys
	CBS			The Witness	Zane Grey Theater
	NBC			The Outlaws	Bat Masterson
Friday	ABC		Matty's Funday Funnies	Harrigan & Son	Flintstones
	CBS			Rawhide	Route 66
	NBC			Dan Raven	The Westerner
Saturday	ABC			Roaring Twenties	Leave It To Beaver
	CBS			Perry Mason	Checkmate
	NBC			Bonanza	The Tall Man

Question 1:
THRILLER was a suspense drama hosted by _____
_____.

NETWORK
SCHEDULE

9PM	9:30	10PM	10:30	11PM		
The Rebel		The Islanders		Walter Winchell Show	ABC	Sunday
G.E. Theater	Jack Benny Show	Candid Camera	What's My Line	CBS	
Dinah Shore Chevy Show		Loretta Young Show	This is Your Life	NBC	
Surfside Six		Adventures in Paradise	Peter Gunn	ABC	Monday
Danny Thomas Show	Andy Griffith Show	Hennesey		CBS	
Klondike	Dante	Barbara Stanwyck Show	Jackpot Bowling	NBC	
Stagecoach West		Alcoa Presents		ABC	Tuesday
Tom Ewell Show	The Red Skelton Show	Garry Moore Show		CBS	
Thriller		Specials		NBC	
Hawaiian Eye		Naked City		ABC	Wednesday
My Sister Eileen	I've Got A Secret	Armstrong Circle Theater/ U.S. Steel Hour		CBS	
Perry Como's Kraft Music Hall		Peter Loves Mary		NBC	
My Three Sons	The Untouchables		Take A Good Look	ABC	Thursday
Angel	Ann Sothern Show	Person to Person	June Allyson Show	CBS	
Bachelor Father	Tennessee Ernie Ford	You Bet Your Life		NBC	
77 Sunset Strip		The Detectives	The Law and Mr. Jones	ABC	Friday
Route 66	Mr. Garland	Twilight Zone	Eye Witness To History	CBS	
Bell Telephone Hour		Michael Shayne		NBC	
Lawrence Welk Show	Fight Of The Week	Make That Spare		ABC	Saturday
Checkmate	Have Gun, Will Travel	Gunsmoke		CBS	
The Deputy	The Nations Future			NBC	

		7PM	7:30	8PM	8:30
Sunday	ABC	Maverick	- Follow The Sun		The Lawman
	CBS	Lassie	Dennis The Menace	The Ed Sullivan Show	
	NBC	Bullwinkle Show	Walt Disney's Wonderful World of Color		Car 54, Where Are You?
Monday	ABC	Cheyenne			The Rifleman
	CBS	To Tell The Truth		Pete & Gladys	Window on Main Street
	NBC	National Velvet			Price Is Right
Tuesday	ABC	Bugs Bunny Show		Bachelor Father	Calvin and The Colonel
	CBS	Marshall Dillon		Dick Van Dyke Show	Dobie Gillis
	NBC	Laramie			Alfred Hitchcock
Wednesday	ABC	Steve Allen Show			Top Cat
	CBS	Alvin Show		Father Knows Best	Checkmate
	NBC	Wagon Train			Joey Bishop Show
Thursday	ABC	Ozzie and Harriet		Donna Reed Show	Real McCoys
	CBS	Frontier Circus			Bob Cummings Show
	NBC	The Outlaws			Doctor Kildare
Friday	ABC	Straight Away		The Hathaways	Flintstones
	CBS	Rawhide			Route 66
	NBC	International Showtime			Robert Taylor's Detectives
Saturday	ABC	Roaring Twenties			Leave It To Beaver
	CBS	Perry Mason			The Lawrence Welk Show
	NBC	Tales of Wells Fargo			The Tall Man

Question 2:
ALCOA PREMIERE was hosted by what very famous movie personality?

NETWORK SCHEDULE

9PM	9:30	10PM	10:30	11PM	
Bus Stop		Adventures in Paradise		ABC	Sunday
G.E. Theater	Jack Benny Show	Candid Camera	What's My Line	CBS	Sunday
Bonanza		DuPont Show of The Week		NBC	Sunday
Surfside Six		Ben Casey		ABC	Monday
Danny Thomas Show	Andy Griffith Show	Hennesey	I've Got A Secret	CBS	Monday
87th Precinct		Thriller		NBC	Monday
New Breed		Alcoa Premiere		ABC	Tuesday
The Red Skelton Show	Ichabod and Me	Garry Moore Show		CBS	Tuesday
Dick Powell Show		Cain's Hundred		NBC	Tuesday
Hawaiian Eye		Naked City		ABC	Wednesday
Checkmate	Mrs. G. Goes To College	Armstrong Circle Theater/ U.S. Steel Hour		CBS	Wednesday
Perry Como's Kraft Music Hall		Bob Newhart Show	David Brinkley's Journal	NBC	Wednesday
My Three Sons	Margie	The Untouchables		ABC	Thursday
The Investigators		CBS Reports		CBS	Thursday
Doctor Kildare	Hazel	Sing Along with Mitch		NBC	Thursday
77 Sunset Strip		Target: The Corruptors		ABC	Friday
Route 66	Father of The Bride	Twilight Zone	Eyewitness	CBS	Friday
Robert Taylor's Detectives	Dinah Shore Show/ Bell Telephone Hour		Here and Now	NBC	Friday
The Lawrence Welk Show		Fight of the Week	Make That Spare	ABC	Saturday
Defenders	Have Gun Will Travel	Gunsmoke		CBS	Saturday
NBC Saturday Night Movie				NBC	Saturday

163

		7PM	7:30	8PM	8:30
Sunday	ABC	Father Knows Best	The Jetsons	ABC Sunday Night Movie	
	CBS	Lassie	Dennis The Menace	The Ed Sullivan Show	
	NBC	Ensign O'Toole	Walt Disney's Wonderful World of Color		Car 54 Where Are You?
Monday	ABC			Cheyenne	Rifleman
	CBS		To Tell The Truth	I've Got a Secret	Lucy Show
	NBC			It's A Man's World	Saints and Sinners
Tuesday	ABC			Combat	Hawaiian Eye
	CBS		Marshal Dillon	Lloyd Bridges Show	The Red Skelton Show
	NBC			Laramie	Empire
Wednesday	ABC			Wagon Train	Going My Way
	CBS			CBS Reports	Dobie Gillis
	NBC		The Virginian		
Thursday	ABC		Ozzie and Harriet	Donna Reed Show	Leave It To Beaver
	CBS		Mr. Ed	Perry Mason	
	NBC			Wide Country	Doctor Kildare
Friday	ABC			Gallant Men	Flintstones
	CBS			Rawhide	Route 66
	NBC			International Showtime	Sing Along with Mitch
Saturday	ABC		Roy Rogers and Dale Evans Show		Mr. Smith Goes to Washington
	CBS		Jackie Gleason Show		The Defenders
	NBC		Sam Benedict		Joey Bishop Show

Question 3:
Who was CANDID CAMERA's co-host?

NETWORK SCHEDULE

9PM	9:30	10PM	10:30	11PM	
ABC Sunday Night Movie		Voice of Firestone	Howard K. Smith	ABC	Sunday
Real McCoys	G.E. True Theater	Candid Camera	What's My Line	CBS	
Bonanza		DuPont Show of The Week		NBC	
Stoney Burke		Ben Casey		ABC	Monday
Danny Thomas Show	Andy Griffith Show	New Loretta Young Show	Stump The Stars	CBS	
Saints and Sinners	Price Is Right	David Brinkley's Journal		NBC	
Hawaiian Eye	The Untouchables		Specials	ABC	Tuesday
The Red Skelton Show	Jack Benny Show	Garry Moore Show		CBS	
Empire	Dick Powell Show		Chet Huntley Reporting	NBC	
Going My Way	Our Man Higgans	Naked City		ABC	Wednesday
Beverly Hillbillies	Dick Van Dyke Show	Armstrong Circle Theater/ U.S. Steel Hour		CBS	
Perry Como's Kraft Music Hall		Eleventh Hour		NBC	
My Three Sons	McHale's Navy	Alcoa Premiere		ABC	Thursday
The Nurses		Alfred Hitchcock		CBS	
Doctor Kildare	Hazel	Andy Williams Show		NBC	
I'm Dickens, He's Fenster	77 Sunset Strip			ABC	Friday
Route 66	Fair Exchange		Eyewitness	CBS	
Sing Along With Mitch	Don't Call Me Charlie	Jack Paar Show		NBC	
Lawrence Welk Show		Fight of The Week	Make That Spare	ABC	Saturday
The Defenders	Have Gun, Will Travel	Gunsmoke		CBS	
NBC Saturday Night Movie				NBC	

		7PM	7:30	8PM	8:30
Sunday	ABC			Travels of Jamie McPheeters	Arrest and Trial
	CBS		Lassie	My Favorite Martian	The Ed Sullivan Show
	NBC		Bill Dana Show	Walt Disney's Wonderful World of Color	Grindle
Monday	ABC			The Outer Limits	Wagon Train
	CBS			To Tell The Truth	I've Got A Secret	Lucy Show
	NBC			NBC Monday Night Movie	
Tuesday	ABC			Combat	McHale's Navy
	CBS			Marshal Dillon	The Red Skelton Show
	NBC			Mr. Novak	Redigo
Wednesday	ABC			Ozzie and Harriet	Patty Duke Show	Price Is Right
	CBS			CBS Reports/Chronicle	Glynis John Show
	NBC			The Virginian	
Thursday	ABC			Flintstones	Donna Reed Show	My Three Sons
	CBS			Password	Rawhide
	NBC			Temple Houston	Doctor
Friday	ABC			77 Sunset Strip	Burke's Law
	CBS			The Great Adventure	Route 66
	NBC			International Showtime	Bob Hope Presents
Saturday	ABC			Hootenanny	Lawrence Welk Show
	CBS			Jackie Gleason Show	Phil Silvers Show
	NBC			The Lieutenant	Joey Bishop Show

Question 4:
What was the background setting for the show
CHANNING?

NETWORK SCHEDULE

9PM	9:30	10PM	10:30	11PM	
Arrest and Trial		100 Grand	ABC News Reports	ABC	Sunday
Judy Garland Show		Candid Camera	What's My Line	CBS	Sunday
Bonanza		DuPont Show of The Week		NBC	Sunday
Wagon Train		Breaking Point		ABC	Monday
Danny Thomas Show	Andy Griffith Show	East Side/West Side		CBS	Monday
Monday Night Movie	Hollywood and The Stars	Sing Along With Mitch		NBC	Monday
Greatest Show on Earth		The Fugitive		ABC	Tuesday
Petticoat Junction	Jack Benny Show	Garry Moore Show		CBS	Tuesday
Richard Boone Show		Bell Telephone Hour		NBC	Tuesday
Ben Casey		Channing		ABC	Wednesday
Beverly Hillbillies	Dick Van Dyke Show	Danny Kay Show		CBS	Wednesday
Espionage		Eleventh Hour		NBC	Wednesday
Jimmy Dean Show		Edie Adams Show/ Sid Caesar Show		ABC	Thursday
Perry Mason		The Nurses		CBS	Thursday
Kildare	Hazel	Kraft Suspense Theater		NBC	Thursday
Burke's Law	The Farmer's Daughter	Fight of The Week	Make That Spare	ABC	Friday
Route 66	Twilight Zone	Alfred Hitchcock		CBS	Friday
The Chrysler Theatre	Harry's Girls	Jack Paar Show		NBC	Friday
Lawrence Welk Show		Jerry Lewis Show		ABC	Saturday
The Defenders		Gunsmoke		CBS	Saturday
NBC Saturday Night Movie				NBC	Saturday

		7PM	7:30	8PM	8:30
Sunday	ABC			Wagon Train	Broadside
	CBS	Lassie		My Favorite Martian	The Ed Sullivan Show
	NBC	Profiles in Courage		Walt Disney's Wonderful World of Color	Bill Dana Show
Monday	ABC			Voyage to the Bottom of the Sea	No Time For Sergeants
	CBS			To Tell The Truth	I've Got A Secret	Andy Griffith Show
	NBC			90 Bristol Court	
Tuesday	ABC			Combat	McHale's Navy
	CBS			Marshal Dillon	World War I	The Red Skelton Show
	NBC			Mr. Novak	Man From U.N.C.L.E.
Wednesday	ABC			Ozzie and Harriet	Patty Duke Show	Shindig
	CBS			CBS Reports	Beverly Hillbillies
	NBC			The Virginian	
Thursday	ABC			Flintstones	Donna Reed Show	My Three Sons
	CBS			The Munsters	Perry Mason
	NBC			Daniel Boone	Doctor Kildare
Friday	ABC			Jonny Quest	The Farmer's Daughter	Addams Family
	CBS			Rawhide	The Entertainers
	NBC			International Showtime	Bob Hope Presents
Saturday	ABC			The Outer Limits	Lawrence Welk Show
	CBS			Jackie Gleason Show	Gilligan's Island
	NBC			Flipper	Mr. Magoo	Kentucky Jones

Question 5:
Each week THAT WAS THE WEEK THAT WAS would satirize the news. The opening and closing of the show was song by the TW3 girl. Who was she?

NETWORK
SCHEDULE

9PM	9:30	10PM	10:30	11PM	
ABC Sunday Night Movie				ABC	Sunday
My Living Doll	Joey Bishop Show	Candid Camera	What's My Line	CBS	
Bonanza			The Rogues	NBC	
Wendy and Me	Bing Crosby Show	Ben Casey		ABC	Monday
Lucy Show	Many Happy Returns	Slattery's People		CBS	
Andy Williams Show		Alfred Hitchcock		NBC	
The Tycoon	Peyton Place	The Fugitive		ABC	Tuesday
The Red Skelton Show	Petticoat Junction	Doctors and The Nurses		CBS	
Man from U.N.C.L.E.	That Was The Week That Was	Bell Telephone Hour/Specials		NBC	
Mickey	Burke's Law		ABC Scope	ABC	Wednesday
Dick Van Dyke Show	Cara Williams Show	Danny Kaye Show		CBS	
NBC Wednesday Night Movie				NBC	
Bewitched	Peyton Place	Jimmy Dean Show		ABC	Thursday
Password	Baileys of Balboa	The Defenders		CBS	
Doctor Kildare	Hazel	Kraft Suspense Theater		NBC	
Valentine's Day	Twelve O'Clock High			ABC	Friday
The Entertainers	Gomer Pyle	The Reporter		CBS	
The Chrysler Theatre	Jack Benny Program	Jack Paar Show		NBC	
Lawrence Welk Show	Hollywood Palace			ABC	Saturday
Mr. Broadway		Gunsmoke		CBS	
NBC Saturday Night Movie				NBC	

		7PM	7:30	8PM	8:30
Sunday	ABC		Voyage to the Bottom of the Sea		The F.B.I.
	CBS	Lassie	My Favorite Martian	The Ed Sullivan Show	
	NBC	Bell Telephone Hour/Specials	Walt Disney's Wonderful World of Color		Branded
Monday	ABC		Twelve O'Clock High		Legend of Jessie James
	CBS		To Tell The Truth	I've Got a Secret	Lucy Show
	NBC		Hullabaloo	John Forsythe Show	Dr. Kildare
Tuesday	ABC		Combat		McHale's Navy
	CBS		Rawhide		The Red Skelton Show
	NBC		My Mother The Car	Please Don't Eat The Daisies	Dr. Kildare
Wednesday	ABC		Ozzie and Harriet	Patty Duke Show	Gidget
	CBS		Lost In Space		Beverly Hillbillies
	NBC		The Virginian		
Thursday	ABC		Shindig	Donna Reed Show	O.K. Crackerby
	CBS		The Munsters	Gilligan's Island	My Three Sons
	NBC		Daniel Boone		Laredo
Friday	ABC		Flintstones	Tammy	Addams Family
	CBS		Wild Wild West		Hogan's Heroes
	NBC		Camp Runamuck	Hank	Convoy
Saturday	ABC		Shindig	King Family	Lawrence Welk Show
	CBS		Jackie Gleason Show		Trials of O'Brien
	NBC		Flipper	I Dream of Jeannie	Get Smart

Question 6:
How many members of the King Family appeared regularly on their musical show?

NETWORK
SCHEDULE

9PM	9:30	10PM	10:30	11PM	
ABC Sunday Night Movie				ABC	Sunday
Perry Mason		Candid Camera	What's My Line	CBS	
Bonanza		Wackiest Ship in the Army		NBC	
A Man Called Shenandoah	The Farmer's Daughter	Ben Casey		ABC	Monday
Andy Griffith Show	Hazel	Steve Lawrence Show		CBS	
Andy Williams Show		Run For Your Life		NBC	
F Troop	Peyton Place	The Fugitive		ABC	Tuesday
The Red Skelton Show	Petticoat Junction	CBS Reports/Specials		CBS	
NBC Tuesday Night Movie				NBC	
Big Valley		Amos Burke—Secret Agent		ABC	Wednesday
Green Acres	Dick Van Dyke Show	Danny Kaye Show		CBS	
Bob Hope Presents the Chrysler Theatre		I Spy		NBC	
Bewitched	Peyton Place	Long Hot Summer		ABC	Thursday
CBS Thursday Night Movie				CBS	
Laredo	Mona McClusky	Dean Martin Show		NBC	
Honey West	Peyton Place	Jimmy Dean Show		ABC	Friday
Gomer Pyle	Smothers Brothers Show	Slattery's People		CBS	
Convoy	Mr. Roberts	Man From U.N.C.L.E.		NBC	
Lawrence Welk Show	Hollywood Palace		ABC Scope	ABC	Saturday
Trials of O'Brian	The Loner	Gunsmoke		CBS	
NBC Saturday Night Movie				NBC	

		7PM	7:30	8PM	8:30
Sunday	ABC	Voyage to the Bottom of the Sea			The F.B.I.
	CBS	Lassie	It's About Time	The Ed Sullivan Show	
	NBC	Bell Telephone Hour Specials	Walt Disney's Wonderful World of Color		Hey Landlord
Monday	ABC	Iron Horse			Rat Patrol
	CBS		Gilligan's Island	Run Buddy Run	Lucy Show
	NBC		The Monkees	I Dream of Jeannie	Roger Miller Show
Tuesday	ABC		Combat		The Rounders
	CBS		Daktari		The Red Skelton Show
	NBC		Girl From U.N.C.L.E.		Occasional Wife
Wednesday	ABC		Batman	The Monroes	
	CBS		Lost In Space		Beverly Hillbillies
	NBC		The Virginian		
Thursday	ABC		Batman	F Troop	Tammy Grimes Show
	CBS		Jericho		My Three Sons
	NBC		Daniel Boone		Star Trek
Friday	ABC		Green Hornet	Time Tunnel	
	CBS		Wild Wild West		Hogan's Heroes
	NBC		Tarzan		Man From U.N.C.L.E.
Saturday	ABC		Shane		Lawrence Welk Show
	CBS		Jackie Gleason Show		Pistols "n" Petticoats
	NBC		Flipper	Please Don't Eat The Daisies	Get Smart

Question 7:
WHAT'S MY LINE began its last season on network television in 1966. Who were the regular panelists?

NETWORK SCHEDULE

9PM	9:30	10PM	10:30	11PM	
ABC Sunday Night Movie				ABC	Sunday
Garry Moore Show		Candid Camera	What's My Line	CBS	Sunday
Bonanza		Andy Williams Show		NBC	Sunday
Felony Squad	Peyton Place	Big Valley		ABC	Monday
Andy Griffith Show	Family Affair	Jean Arthur Show	I've Got A Secret	CBS	Monday
Road West		Run For Your Life		NBC	Monday
Pruitts of Southampton	Love on A Rooftop	The Fugitive		ABC	Tuesday
The Red Skelton Show	Petticoat Junction	CBS Reports/Specials		CBS	Tuesday
NBC Tuesday Night Movie				NBC	Tuesday
The Man Who Never Was	Peyton Place	ABC Stage 67		ABC	Wednesday
Green Acres	Gomer Pyle	Danny Kaye Show		CBS	Wednesday
Bob Hope Presents The Chrysler Theatre		I Spy		NBC	Wednesday
Bewitched	That Girl	Hawk		ABC	Thursday
CBS Thursday Night Movie				CBS	Thursday
Star Trek	The Hero	Dean Martin Show		NBC	Thursday
Milton Berle Show		Twelve O'clock High		ABC	Friday
CBS Friday Night Movie				CBS	Friday
Man from U.N.C.L.E.	T.H.E. Cat	Laredo		NBC	Friday
Lawrence Welk Show	Hollywood Palace	ABC Scope		ABC	Saturday
Mission Impossible		Gunsmoke		CBS	Saturday
NBC Saturday Night Movie				NBC	Saturday

173

		7PM	7:30	8PM	8:30
Sunday	ABC		Voyage to the Bottom of the Sea		The F.B.I.
	CBS	Lassie	Gentle Ben	The Ed Sullivan Show	
	NBC		Walt Disney's Wonderful World of Color		Mothers-in-Law
Monday	ABC		Cowboy in Africa		Rat Patrol
	CBS		Gunsmoke		Lucy Show
	NBC		The Monkees	Man From U.N.C.L.E.	
Tuesday	ABC		Garrison's Gorillas		The Invaders
	CBS		Daktari		The Red Skelton Show
	NBC		I Dream of Jeannie	Jerry Lewis Show	
Wednesday	ABC		Legend of Custer		Second 100 Years
	CBS		Lost In Space		Beverly Hillbillies
	NBC		The Virginian		
Thursday	ABC		Batman	Flying Nun	Bewitched
	CBS		Cimarron Strip		
	NBC		Daniel Boone		Ironside
Friday	ABC		Off To See The Wizard		Hondo
	CBS		Wild Wild West		Gomer Pyle
	NBC		Tarzan		Star Trek
Saturday	ABC		Dating Game	Newlywed Game	Lawrence Welk Show
	CBS		Jackie Gleason Show		My Three Sons
	NBC		Maya		Get Smart

Question 8:
Where did the adventure series MAYA take place?

NETWORK SCHEDULE

9PM	9:30	10PM	10:30	11PM	Day
ABC Sunday Night Movie				ABC	Sunday
Smothers Brothers Comedy Hour		Mission Impossible		CBS	Sunday
Bonanza		High Chaparral		NBC	Sunday
Felony Squad	Peyton Place	Big Valley		ABC	Monday
Andy Griffith Show	Family Affair	Carol Burnett Show		CBS	Monday
Danny Thomas Hour		I Spy		NBC	Monday
The Invaders	N.Y.P.D.	Hollywood Palace		ABC	Tuesday
The Red Skelton Show	Good Morning World	CBS Reports/Specials		CBS	Tuesday
NBC Tuesday Night Movie				NBC	Tuesday
ABC Wednesday Night Movie				ABC	Wednesday
Green Acres	He & She	Dundee and the Culhane		CBS	Wednesday
Kraft Music Hall		Run For Your Life		NBC	Wednesday
That Girl	Peyton Place	Good Company		ABC	Thursday
CBS Thursday Night Movie				CBS	Thursday
Ironside	Dragnet	Dean Martin Show		NBC	Thursday
Hondo	Guns of Will Sonnett	Judd for the Defense		ABC	Friday
CBS Friday Night Movie				CBS	Friday
Star Trek	Accidental Family	Bell Telephone Hour/Specials		NBC	Friday
Lawrence Welk Show	Iron Horse		ABC Scope	ABC	Saturday
Hogan's Heroes	Petticoat Junction	Mannix		CBS	Saturday
NBC Saturday Night Movie				NBC	Saturday

	7PM	7:30	8PM	8:30
Sunday ABC	Land Of The Giants			The F.B.I.
CBS	Lassie	Gentle Ben	The Ed Sullivan Show	
NBC	New Adventures of Huck Finn	Walt Disney's Wonderful World of Color		Mothers-in-Law
Monday ABC		The Avengers		Peyton Place
CBS		Gunsmoke		Here's Lucy
NBC		I Dream of Jeannie	Rowan & Martin's Laugh-In	
Tuesday ABC		Mod Squad		It Takes A Thief
CBS		Lancer		The Red Skelton Show
NBC		Jerry Lewis Show		Julia
Wednesday ABC		Here Come The Brides		Peyton Place
CBS		Daktari		Good Guys
NBC		The Virginian		
Thursday ABC		Ugliest Girl in Town	Flying Nun	Bewitched
CBS		Blondie	Hawaii Five-O	
NBC		Daniel Boone		Ironsides
Friday ABC		Operation Entertainment		Felony Squad
CBS		Wild Wild West		Gomer Pyle
NBC		High Chaparral		Name of the Game
Saturday ABC		Dating Game	Newlywed Game	Lawrence Welk Show
CBS		Jackie Gleason Show		My Three Sons
NBC		Adam-12	Get Smart	Ghost and Mrs Muir

Question 9:
Robert Morse of HOW TO SUCCEED IN BUSINESS WITHOUT REALLY TRYING fame starred in what series this year?

NETWORK SCHEDULE

9PM	9:30	10PM	10:30	11PM	
ABC Sunday Night Movie				ABC	Sunday
Smothers Brothers Comedy Hour		Mission Impossible		CBS	
Bonanza		Beautiful Phyllis Diller Show		NBC	
The Outcasts		Big Valley		ABC	Monday
Mayberry R.F.D.	Family Affair	Carol Burnett Show		CBS	
NBC Monday Night Movie				NBC	
It Takes A Thief	N.Y.P.D.	That's Life		ABC	Tuesday
The Red Skelton Show	Doris Day Show	60 Minutes/Specials		CBS	
NBC Tuesday Night Movie				NBC	
ABC Wednesday Night Movie				ABC	Wednesday
Beverly Hillbillies	Green Acres	Jonathan Winters Show		CBS	
Kraft Music Hall		The Outsider		NBC	
That Girl	Journey To The Unknown			ABC	Thursday
CBS Thursday Night Movie				CBS	
Ironside	Dragnet	Dean Martin Show		NBC	
Don Rickles Show	Guns of Will Sonnett	Judd for the Defense		ABC	Friday
CBS Friday Night Movie				CBS	
Name of the Game		Star Trek		NBC	
Lawrence Welk Show	Hollywood Palace			ABC	Saturday
Hogan's Heroes	Petticoat Junction	Mannix		CBS	
NBC Saturday Night Movie				NBC	

		7PM	7:30	8PM	8:30
Sunday	ABC	Land Of The Giants			The F.B.I.
	CBS	Lassie	To Rome With Love	The Ed Sullivan Show	
	NBC	Wild Kingdom	Walt Disney's Wonderful World of Color		Bill Cosby Show
Monday	ABC		Music Scene		New People
	CBS		Gunsmoke		Here's Lucy
	NBC		My World and Welcome To It	Rowan & Martin's Laugh-In	
Tuesday	ABC		Mod Squad		Movie of the Week
	CBS		Lancer		The Red Skelton Show
	NBC		I Dream of Jeannie	Debbie Reynolds Show	Julia
Wednesday	ABC		Flying Nun	Courtship of Eddie's Father	Room 222
	CBS		Glen Campbell Goodtime Hour		Beverly Hillbillies
	NBC		The Virginian		
Thursday	ABC		Ghost and Mrs. Muir	That Girl	Bewitched
	CBS		Family Affair	Jim Nabors Hour	
	NBC		Daniel Boone		Ironside
Friday	ABC		Lets Make A Deal	Brady Bunch	Mr. Deeds Goes To Town
	CBS		Get Smart	Good Guys	Hogan's Heroes
	NBC		High Chaparral		Name of the Game
Saturday	ABC		Dating Game	Newlywed Game	Lawrence Welk Show
	CBS		Jackie Gleason Show		My Three Sons
	NBC		Andy Williams Show		Adam-12

Question 10:
Who was the announcer long associated with the
KRAFT MUSIC HALL program?

NETWORK SCHEDULE

9PM	9:30	10PM	10:30	11PM	
ABC Sunday Night Movie				ABC	Sunday
Leslie Uggams Show		Mission Impossible		CBS	
Bonanza		Bold Ones		NBC	
The Survivors		Love American Style		ABC	Monday
Mayberry R.F.D.	Doris Day Show	Carol Burnett Show		CBS	
NBC Monday Night Movie				NBC	
Movie of the Week		Marcus Welby, M.D.		ABC	Tuesday
The Red Skelton Show	Governor and J.J.	60 Minutes/Specials		CBS	
NBC Tuesday Night Movie				NBC	
ABC Wednesday Night Movie				ABC	Wednesday
Medical Center		Hawaii Five-O		CBS	
Kraft Music Hall		Then Came Bronson		NBC	
This Is Tom Jones		It Takes a Thief		ABC	Thursday
CBS Thursday Night Movie				CBS	
Ironside	Dragnet	Dean Martin Show		NBC	
Here Come The Brides		Jimmy Durante Presents The Lennon Sisters		ABC	Friday
CBS Friday Night Movie				CBS	
Name of the Game		Bracken's World		NBC	
Lawrence Welk Show	Hollywood Palace			ABC	Saturday
Green Acres	Petticoat Junction	Mannix		CBS	
NBC Saturday Night Movie				NBC	

ANSWERS

1960

1. U.S. STEEL HOUR — "Queen Of The Orange Bowl"
2. MALIBU RUN
3. Bill Williams and Diane Mountford
4. BRINGING UP BUDDY — Frank Aletter
5. Anthony George, Doug McClure and Sebastian Cabot
6. THE CLEAR HORIZONS
7. DAN RAVEN
8. THE FLINTSTONES
9. GUESTWARD HO! — Mark Miller and Joanne Dru
10. HARRIGAN AND SON — Pat O'Brien and Roger Perry
11. Rod Taylor — HONG KONG
12. THE ISLANDERS
13. James Coburn — KLONDIKE
14. James Whitmore
15. MAN FROM INTERPOL
16. MY SISTER EILEEN — Elaine Stritch and Shirley Boone

17. Tim Considine was Mike, the eldest
    Don Grady was Robbie
    Stanley Livingston was Chip, the youngest
18. NATIONAL VELVET — Lori Martin
19. THE OVERLAND TRAIL — Doug McClure
20. Harry Morgan and Cara Williams
21. THE ROARING TWENTIES — Donald May, Rex
    Reason, and Dorothy Provine
22. Tod Stiles and Buzz Murdock/Martin Milner and
    George Maharis
23. TATE
24. Tab Hunter — THE TAB HUNTER SHOW

1961

1. Jim McKay — April 29, 1961
2. THE ALVIN SHOW — CBS
3. THE AMERICANS
4. THE ASPHALT JUNGLE — Jack Warden and Arch Johnson
5. Dr. Daniel Freeland/Franchot Tone
6. BUS STOP — Marilyn Miller
7. CAIN'S HUNDRED — Mark Richman
8. Officer Gunther Toody and Officer Francis Muldoon — Joe E. Ross and Fred Gwynne
9. DANGER MAN — Patrick McGoohan
10. THE DEFENDERS — E. G. Marshall, Robert Reed
11. The Alan Brady Show
12. Dr. Leonard Gillespie — Blair General Hospital
13. Robert Lansing — she was a deaf mute — Gena Rowlands
14. Banks — Fairview Mannor, Connecticut
15. Chill Wills, John Derek — FRONTIER CIRCUS
16. GREAT GHOST TALES
17. GUNSLINGER — Preston Foster
18. Jack Weston and Peggy Cass
19. Hazel Burke — The Baxter Family

20. Allan "Rocky" Lane, previously a western star
21. ONE HAPPY FAMILY — Dick Sargent and Jody Warner
22. TALLAHASSEE 7000
23. TARGET: THE CORRUPTORS — Stephen McNally
24. Joe Shannon — SHANNON

1962

1. Vic Morrow and Rick Jason — COMBAT — ABC
2. Dean Jones — USS Appleby
3. Lynn Loring and Judy Carne
4. I'M DICKENS, HE'S FENSTER — John Astin played Harry Dickens, Marty Ingels played Arch Fenster.
5. Area 1 — The Island of Taratupa in the South Pacific. Area 2 — Voltafiore, a small town in southern Italy
6. MR. SMITH GOES TO WASHINGTON — Fess Parker
7. Loretta Young — THE NEW LORETTA YOUNG SHOW
8. Shirl Conway and Zina Bethune
9. OUR MAN HIGGINS
10. Ken Curtis
11. Andrew Duggan and Peggy McCay
12. SAINTS AND SINNERS
13. SAM BENEDICT
14. Jack Lord — "The Gold Buckle"
15. THE VIRGINIAN — James Drury and Doug McClure
16. WIDE COUNTRY — Earl Holliman and Andrew Prine

17. Captain James Benedict/William Reynolds and Correspondent Conley Wright/Robert McQueeny
18. MAGIC MIDWAY
19. Craig Stevens
20. Sir Francis Drake
21. THE BEACHCOMBER — Cameron Mitchell
22. GOING MY WAY — Gene Kelly and Leo G. Carroll
23. TELL IT TO GROUCHO
24. YOUR FIRST IMPRESSION

1963

1. Ben Gazzara as the police detective, Chuck Connors as the public defender
2. BATTLE LINE
3. BREAKING POINT — York Hospital
4. CBS — four years
5. EAST SIDE, WEST SIDE — George C. Scott
6. THE FARMER'S DAUGHTER — Inger Stevens and William Windom
7. Diane Brewster
8. THE GREATEST SHOW ON EARTH — Jack Palance and Stu Erwin
9. Imogene Coca
10. THE HECTOR HEATHCOTE SHOW
11. Jefferson High School — Albert Vane
12. Harry Grafton — plant foreman
13. Temple Houston — TEMPLE HOUSTON
14. José Jimenez — THE BILL DANA SHOW
15. A) BURKE'S LAW B) Amos Burke C) Rolls Royce D) Gene Barry
16. ABC
17. Joseph Cotton
18. Jack Linkletter

19. THE DOCTORS — NBC, GENERAL HOSPITAL
    — ABC; April 1, 1963
20. WILD KINGDOM — NBC
21. THE LIEUTENANT — Gary Lockwood and Robert
    Vaughn
22. Ed McMahon — Dick Clark
23. THE DAKOTAS
24. Merv Griffin

1964

1. THE MINNOW
2. THE BAILEYS OF BALBOA
3. BROADSIDE
4. Mingo/Ed Ames
5. United Network Command for Law and Enforcement
6. MANY HAPPY RETURNS — John McGiver
7. MR. BROADWAY — Craig Stevens
8. Beverly Owen — Pat Priest
9. David Niven, Charles Boyer, Gig Young, and Robert Coote
10. SLATTERY'S PEOPLE
11. David Hedison, Bob Dowdell
12. Pugsley and Wednesday/Ken Weatherwax and Lisa Loring
13. Cara Williams and Frank Aletter — THE CARA WILLIAMS SHOW
14. Brian Kelly
15. Bing Crosby
16. KENTUCKY JONES — Kenneth (Kentucky) Yarborough Jones
17. Les Crane

18. Mickey Rooney, Timmy Rooney — MICKEY
19. Jim Backus
20. Rhoda was a robot, designed to think like a human being — MY LIVING DOLL
21. Will Stockdale — Sammy Jackson — Air Force
22. ABC — Tuesday and Thursday
23. PROFILES IN COURAGE
24. Tony Franciosa — VALENTINE'S DAY

1965

1. CAMP RUNAMUCK
2. CONVOY
3. Captain Wilton Parmenter/Ken Berry
4. FOR THE PEOPLE
5. C.O.N.T.R.O.L. — K.A.O.S.
6. GIDGET — Sally Field
7. Honey West/Anne Francis
8. Robert Culp, Bill Cosby — I SPY
9. June Lockhart and Guy Williams
10. Robert Horton
11. MONA McCLUSKEY
12. Melinda Plank and Carol Gainer
13. Burl Ives
14. Pretty Darn Quick
15. Patricia Crowley and Mark Miller
16. Paul Bryan — RUN FOR YOUR LIFE
17. TRIALS OF O'BRIAN
18. *Kiwi*, THE WACKIEST SHIP IN THE ARMY, Jack Warden, Gary Collins
19. Ulysses S. Grant
20. THE BIG VALLEY — Barbara Stanwyck
21. Nine

22. Sunday — eight — ABC
23. GREEN ACRES — Eddie Albert and Eva Gabor/ Oliver and Lisa Douglas
24. HULLABALOO — NBC

1966

1. THE DOUBLE LIFE OF HENRY PHYFE — Red Buttons
2. THE FACE IS FAMILIAR
3. Stefanie Powers — April Dancer
4. THE GREEN HORNET — Van Williams
5. THE IRON HORSE — Dale Robertson
6. JERICHO
7. LOVE ON A ROOFTOP — Judy Carne and Peter Deuel
8. Davy Jones, Mike Nesmith, Mickey Dolenz, Peter Tork
9. Ann Sheridan — PISTOLS 'N' PETTICOATS
10. Phyllis Diller — THE PRUITTS OF SOUTHAMPTON
11. THE RAT PATROL — Christopher George
12. David Carradine
13. Thomas Hewitt Edward Cat
14. Brewster, New York
15. THE TIME TUNNEL — James Darren and Robert Colbert
16. BLUE LIGHT — Robert Goulet

17. FELONY SQUAD — Dennis Cole and Ben Alexander
18. THE HERO — Richard Mulligan
19. IT'S ABOUT TIME — Frank Aletter and Jack Mullaney
20. OCCASIONAL WIFE
21. THE TAMMY GRIMES SHOW
22. A) Cesar Romero B) Burgess Meredith C) Frank Gorshin D) Art Carney E) Tallulah Bankhead F) Vincent Price G) Van Johnson H) Roddy McDowall I) Victor Buono J) Michael Rennie
23. RUN, BUDDY RUN — Sheldon
24. Documentary (comedy)

1967

1. ACCIDENTAL FAMILY — Jerry Van Dyke
2. George Carlin
3. Police chemist — CAPTAIN NICE — William Daniels
4. CIMARRON STRIP
5. COWBOY IN AFRICA — Chuck Connors
6. Wayne Maunder
7. John Mills and Sean Garrison
8. Elsie Ethrington
9. GARRISON'S GORILLAS
10. GOOD MORNING WORLD — Joby Baker
11. Richard Benjamin — Paula Prentiss — HE & SHE
12. Cannon and Montoya
13. Regis Philbin
14. JUDD FOR THE DEFENSE
15. LOVE IS A MANY SPLENDORED THING
16. Stephen Strimpell — MR. TERRIFIC
17. THE MOTHERS-IN-LAW
18. RANGO — Tim Conway
19. THE SECOND HUNDRED YEARS — Monte Markham
20. Ed McMahon, — NBC

21. Peter Parker
22. Eleven
23. Ralph Taeger
24. THE FAMILY GAME — Bob Barker

1968

1. Patricia Harty and Will Hutchins
2. Stuart Damon, Alexandra Bastedo, William Gaunt
3. Captain David Gregg/Edward Mulhare
4. THE GOOD GUYS — Herb Edelman, Bob Denver, and Joyce Van Patten
5. THE GUNS OF WILL SONNETT — Walter Brennan and Dack Rambo
6. Noah Bain — Malachi Throne
7. Andrew Duggan, Wayne Maunder, and James Stacy
8. Pete Cochran . . . . Michael Cole
   Linc Hayes . . . . Clarence Williams III
   Julie Barnes . . . . Peggy Lipton
9. Glenn Howard . . Publisher . . . . Gene Barry
   Jeff Dilloh . . . . . . Investigative reporter . . . . . Tony Franciosa
   Dan Farrell . . . . . Senior Editor . . . . . Robert Stack
10. THE OUTCASTS — Don Murray and Otis Young
11. THE OUTSIDER — Darren McGavin
12. PREMIERE
13. Julia Baker . . . . . Diahann Carrol
    Corey . . . . Marc Copage
14. MAN IN A SUIT CASE — Robert Bradford

15. Ken Berry/Sam Jones — Buddy Foster/Mike
16. OPERATION: ENTERTAINMENT
17. THE PRISONER — Patrick McGoohan
18. Mike Wallace and Harry Reasoner
19. Peter Kastner — THE UGLIEST GIRL IN TOWN
20. Officer Pete Malloy and Officer Jim Reed
21. Richard Hays
22. THE BEAUTIFUL PHYLLIS DILLER SHOW
23. Mike Darrow
24. THE GOLDDIGGERS

1969

1. Leslie Nielsen
2. THE COURTSHIP OF EDDIE'S FATHER — Bill Bixby and Brandon Cruz
3. Dan Dailey and Julie Sommars
4. MARCUS WELBY, M.D. and MEDICAL CENTER
5. William Windom — MY WORLD AND WELCOME TO IT
6. Lloyd Haynes — Walt Whitman High School
7. THE SURVIVORS — Lana Turner
8. THEN CAME BRONSON — Michael Parks
9. Bill Cosby — THE BILL COSBY SHOW
10. BRIGHT PROMISE
11. Monte Markham — MR. DEEDS GOES TO TOWN
12. MY FRIEND TONY — James Whitmore, Enzo Cerusico
13. THE MUSIC SCENE and THE NEW PEOPLE
14. THE QUEEN AND I — *Amsterdam Queen*
15. SCOOBY-DOO, WHERE ARE YOU?
16. TURN-ON — one telecast
17. THE NEW DOCTORS — THE LAWYERS — THE PROTECTORS — THE SENATOR

THE 1960s PHOTO AND PROGRAM SCHEDULE ANSWERS

Photo Answers

1. Opie — Mayberry, North Carolina
2. 53rd Precinct
3. Millie and Jerry Helper
4. Wednesday
5. COMBAT — five years
6. John Larch and Chuck Connors — ARREST AND TRIAL
7. Bradley — Hooterville
8. 1313 Mockingbird Lane
9. Lieutenant Gerard
10. Edward Platt
11. FAMILY AFFAIR — Bill Davis
12. Dan Briggs
13. Woody Woodbury
14. Richard Denning
15. Tiger, the family dog

Program Schedule Answers

1. Boris Karloff
2. Fred Astaire
3. Durwood Kirby
4. Channing College
5. Nancy Ames
6. Thirty-six
7. Arlene Francis and Bennett Cerf
8. India
9. THAT'S LIFE
10. Ed Herlihy

The 1970s

QUESTIONS

1970

1. The problems and pitfalls of a loading dock foreman who is uprooted and thrust into the executive suite made for many comical events in this series. Name the program, the character's full name and the star.
2. Scoey Mitchell and Tracy Reed were the stars of this situation comedy that only lasted half a season. The story was first a successful Broadway show and then a popular movie. Name this ill-fated television series.
3. Flip Wilson, who hosted his own variety show for four years, created several characters that became very popular with the American television audience. Can you name these characters?
4. HOT DOG was a program which regularly featured Woody Allen, Jonathan Winters, and Jo-Anne Worley. What type of a show was it?
5. THE INTERNS was a hospital dramatic series about the lives of a group of young doctors under the direction of a senior physician. Who played the senior physician?
6. Each week in an hour-long detective series, a master

criminologist and his two protegés solved a very difficult and complex murder case. What was the name of this show?

7. Monday night NFL football began in 1970. Who were the original commentators?

8. Shirley Partridge, the widowed head of the Partridge clan, had five children. Can you name them?

9. Amelia Cole, Ward Fuller, and Jason Hart were government undercover agents in this thirty-minute law enforcement series. What was the name of this series?

10. _____ _____ had the misfortune of starring in two different shows this year that failed.

11. An interesting historical adventure series revolved around the activities of the Yankee Doodle Society, an organization comprised of young American patriots who did whatever was necessary to thwart the British in the Revolutionary War era. Can you name this show?

12. The neighborhood law office was the setting where free legal aid was available to people who could not afford an attorney in this interesting drama series. What actor played the lead role and do you recall the name of the series?

13. Comic Louis Nye hosted an hour-long summer variety show about the 1930s and 1940s. What was the name of this nostalgic show?

14. Andy Thompson was the principal of a private coeducational high school in this weekly series. Do you know the star and name of this series?

15. Several years after Ben Casey, Vince Edwards starred in another medical series. Can you name the series and the character's medical specialty?

16. Dennis Weaver played McCloud, the Deputy Marshal from Taos, New Mexico on assignment with the New York City Police Department in the series of the same name. Who was McCloud's boss, and what actor played that role?

17. What was the name of and who starred in the comedy

series about the U.S. president's daughter who was in love with a midwestern veterinarian?

18. Phobe Figalilly, better known as _____, housekeeper to the Everett family, was played by _____ _____ in the comedy series _____ _____ ___ _____.

19. Jack Klugman and Tony Randall were THE ODD COUPLE, but who was the only other featured character in the series throughout its entire run, and who played the role?

20. Jack Brennan was a state department employee assigned to the U.S. Embassy in Paris to help Americans in trouble. Who played this role and what was the name of this mystery series?

21. A CBS prime-time cartoon show, about a football team, featured the voices of Cliff Norton and Mel Blanc, was titled _____ ____.

22. FOUR-IN-ONE was the overall title for four different series on the NBC television network. Can you name the four series?

23. David Hansen, Deborah Sullivan and Gabe Kaye were the three principal characters in what dramatic series about lawyers?

24. Soap opera buffs were delighted on one particular day in 1970 because three new daytime serials began. Can you name them and the day they commenced?

1971

1. Line McCray and his Uncle Latzi were partners in a speakeasy during prohibition. Episodes centered around their efforts to keep the big-time gangsters from taking them over in this comedy series. What was the name of this series?

2. Paul Ryan was the Deputy District Attorney and "Staff" Stafford was the Chief Deputy District Attorney in an interesting courtroom drama. Who played the characters mentioned and what was the name of the series?

3. Tired of continuing economic problems, mortgage bills, car loans, etc., Albert and Jane Miller decide to become household domestics for a very wealthy industrialist and attempt to get a taste of the "good life." What was the name of this comedy series and who were the stars?

4. _____ _____ hosted a half-hour nostalgic documentary show about the earlier years of the twentieth century titled IT WAS A VERY GOOD YEAR.

5. _____ was the title of an hour-long crime drama about a New Orleans insurance investigator, played by ___ _____ who usually solved whatever case he was on, even though he was left _____ from an attack on his life.

6. Mayor Thomas Jefferson Alcala was the principal character in the drama series ___ ___ ___ ___ ___ starring _____ _____.

7. OWEN MARSHALL, COUNSELOR AT LAW was a series about lawyers that starred ___ _____ and _____ _____.

8. Lennie Crooke and George Robinson were two inept detectives who were constantly getting themselves into trouble in this police comedy series. What was the name of the series?

9. Tony Curtis and Roger Moore were two wealthy playboys who decided to pool their talents as an investigative team to fight crime in a weekly adventure series. Can you name this adventure series?

10. What was the name of the half-hour show Betty White hosted on which wildlife preservation and ecology were discussed, and celebrities and their pets appeared?

11. An underwater adventure series about the cases of an oceanographer was titled _____ starring ___ _____.

12. Who was the star of SARGE, the story of a policeman turned priest?

13. This comedy series starred a major film actress in the role of a photojournalist who traveled around the globe on assignments. What was the name of the program and star?

14. Chad Smith was a twenty-five year veteran on the Los Angeles police force in this family comedy show. Who played Chad Smith and what was the name of the series?

15. Whoo Poo and Weenie The Genie were characters on what Saturday morning children's adventure program?

16. MAKE YOUR OWN TYPE OF MUSIC was a summer variety show hosted by a brother and sister singing team. Who were they?

17. Dick Preston was a local television talk-show host living in Phoenix, Arizona with his wife Jenny, during the first two seasons this comedy series was on the

air. Who played Dick and Jenny and what was the name of the show?

18. Rod Taylor and Dennis Cole teamed up as a couple of adventurers in the southwest around 1914 in this short-lived series. Can you name the series?

19. Who played Senior Deputy J.J. Jackson in the modern western series CADE'S COUNTY?

20. A comedy series about songwriters trying to "make it" was titled _____ _____ and starred _____ _____ and _____ _____.

21. Susan Saint James was married to Rock Hudson in McMILLAN AND WIFE, but who played the commissioner's chief aide and what was his name?

22. What was the name of the prime-time quiz show that used film clips to verify contestants' answers, and who hosted the program?

23. Who was the star of the comedy series FUNNY FACE?

24. Johnny Olsen, popular announcer on many game shows, did the same on THE MEMORY GAME, but who was the host?

1972

1. BRIDGET LOVES BERNIE was an ethnic comedy about a Jewish boy falling in love with a rich Irish girl. Who played the roles of the parents?
2. Don Robinson was a New York advertising executive with countless problems which he never seemed to be able to solve in this short-lived comedy series. Can you name the program and star?
3. EMERGENCY was a medical drama about a group of paramedics assigned to the Los Angeles Fire Department. What was the name of the doctor at the hospital who usually gave the paramedic team their life-saving instructions and what actor portrayed the role?
4. KUNG FU was a philosophical series in a western setting and starred David Carradine. What was the full name of the character he played?
5. Hugh Lockwood, Nick Bianco, and C.R. Grover were all agents for Probe, ultra-sophisticated investigative agency. Name the actors who played these characters and the program.
6. Each week Dr. Michael Rhodes was involved in some drama in which extrasensory perception, telepathy, and other psychic phenomina were an integral part of

the story. What was the name of the program and who was the star?

7. Detective Lieutenant Mike _____, played by _____ _____, and Inspector _____ Keller, played by _____ _____, made up the team that worked together on the popular police series _____ _____ _____ _____ _____.

8. S.H.A.D.O. was an acronym for an investigative organization in this science fiction series. Define S.H.A.D.O. and name the science fiction series.

9. ANNA AND THE KING was based on the hit Broadway play and movie "The King And I," starring Yul Brynner. In the television series Yul Brynner recreated his role as the King, but who played Anna?

10. Private eye Mike Banyon had a tough time staying in the detective business in Los Angeles during the impoverished 1930s. Who starred as BANYON?

11. The main characters in a Saturday morning cartoon series similar to ALL IN THE FAMILY were a family of _____ and was titled _____ _____.

12. Bob Newhart was a psychologist in his comedy series, but can you recall the name of the orthodontist who shared the same floor with him and the actor who played the role?

13. Dr. Dean Jamison and his daughter and partner Dr. Anne Jamison were two pediatricians in this comedy program which took place in Hawaii. Name the series and the stars.

14. Mike Reynolds was a dentist whose children persuaded him to let them keep a runaway chimpanzee in this weekly comedy series. Can you name the program and who played the dentist?

15. Dr. Simon Locke, played by _____ _____, was the principal character in this crime drama series _____ _____.

16. Three private detectives, American, British, and French, combined their talents in this adventure series which took place in Europe. What was the name of this show?

17. THE ROOKIES was a popular police series which

gave insight into how new policeman develop on the job. Who originally played the roles of the rookies?

18. Sandy Duncan starred in a show bearing her own name, about a student teacher and part-time secretary employed by an advertising agency. Who played the part of her employer on the show?

19. Tom Kennedy hosted many quiz shows over the years. The format for this particular show was such that contestants had very little time to think about their answers. Speed was essential. What was the name of the show?

20. In 1972 a medical series, YOUNG DR. KILDARE, based on the very popular DR. KILDARE program of the 1960s, made its appearance debut. Who played the principal roles in the new series?

21. What was the name of the apartment building superintendent on THE SUPER, and who played him?

22. Paul Lynde starred in a situation comedy bearing his own name and played the role of Paul Simms. What was his occupation?

23. What was the name of the three weekly rotating adventure series which were presented under the overall title of THE MEN?

24. GAMBIT was a daytime game show. Who was the host?

1973

1. ADAM'S RIB was a comedy series based on the movie of the same name about a husband, an assistant district attorney, and his wife, an attorney, Many times because of their jobs they had opposing points of view in a courtroom. Who were the stars of this show?
2. Joe Calucci, played by ____ ____, was the supervisor of a ____ ____ ____ in this short-lived situation comedy series ____ ____.
3. Sally Burton was a new bride who made her husband aware that she had E.S.P. and was able to read his mind as well as others. This of course led to many amusing and embarrassing situations. Name the comedy series and the actress who played Sally Burton.
4. Lorne Greene played the part of a ____ in ____, his first television series after BONANZA.
5. Jimmy Stewart played the part of ____ ____ ____, a country lawyer, in the ninety-minute crime series ____.
6. What was the made-for-television movie that was the pilot for the hit police series KOJAK?
7. Stanley Belmont was a clerk in the lost and found department of the New York City Bus Line Com-

212

pany. In what comedy series is this character found and who played the role?

8. THE NEW PERRY MASON series had little success and was cancelled after fifteen episodes. Who played the following roles:
   A) Perry Mason B) Della Street C) Hamilton Burger D) Lieutenant Tragg

9. A brother, sister, pickle factory, and a $75,000 inheritance were the elements which went into this family comedy series. Name the stars and program.

10. TOMA was a police series about the exploits of a real cop. Who played this real-life character?

11. A widow and her boyfriend, a gravedigger, were the principals in this situation comedy titled __ ___ ___ _____ starring ___ _____ and __ ___ _____.

12. Police departments have special units that are used from time to time for unusual cases. This series concerned itself with these units and starred Mitchell Ryan. Name the series.

13. Jack Parr, after a long absence, returned to late-night television on a one week per month basis. Who was Jack Parr's announcer and sidekick?

14. What was the name of the sitcom about a black man and white man working for the same company and then becoming next-door neighbors?

15. An extraordinary documentary series recording the everyday living of a California family was shown on public television. What was the name of the family and the series?

16. Diana Smythe, recently divorced, arrived in New York from London to begin a new life and career in this short-run series. Who played Diana Smythe and what was the name of this program?

17. What was the name of the Saturday morning cartoon series on NBC that featured the world's smallest detective?

18. Another wacky World War II comedy series, this time about a mostly black quartermaster outfit, was titled ____ _____.

19. A wagon train heading west with Bob Denver and

Forrest Tucker in charge; so you can image the comedy that prevailed. Name this western series.

20. Ozzie and Harriet Nelson, many years after their children grew up and were out of the house, decided to rent their boys' room to two college girls. What was the name of this program?

21. What were the first names of THE SNOOP SISTERS and who played them?

22. BOB AND CAROL AND TED AND ALICE was a little too progressive for television and was cancelled after a few episodes. Who played Bob, Carol, Ted, and Alice?

23. A New York doctor gave up his lucrative practice for life in a small Colorado town. Name the series and star.

24. NBC was the first network to commence late-late-night television (after 1 A.M.) by introducing two programs during 1973. Name the two shows and the nights they appeared.

1974

1. George Apple was an architect living in a large metropolitan city who decided to move with his family back to the small town where he was born. This general drama deals with the many problems he and his family encountered while readjusting their lives. Who played George Apple and what was the name of this series?

2. BORN FREE was an adventure series about the true-life experiences of East African game wardens, George and Joy Adamson. What actors portrayed them in this television series?

3. CHOPPER ONE was about police department helicopter pilots and their experiences. Who were the stars of this police series?

4. A crusty old lady and a young ex-gunfighter team up and become traveling companions in their mutual desire to reach the gold fields of California in this western series. What was the name of this show?

5. A drama series about firefighters was titled _____, and starred ____ _____ in the role of Captain Spike Ryerson.

6. Harry Orwell was a cop who was injured in the line of duty and forced to retire. Naturally, he then become a

private detective. Who played Harry Orwell and what was the title of this program?

7. Contestants could win up to $50,000 by answering riddles correctly on what daytime quiz show?

8. This weekly drama series had a sensitive story line about the relationship between a teacher and his students. What was the name of the program and who starred?

9. Dave Barrett was an amateur crime fighter and bounty hunter during the depression years of the 1930s in this weekly crime drama. Who played Dave Barrett and what was the name of this program?

10. Two truckers, ____ _____ and ____ _____, were the principal characters on MOVIN' ON.

11. A big-city lawyer gives up his practice to settle and work in a small southwestern town. This was the background for what hour-long dramatic series and who was the star?

12. Angie Dickinson starred as Sergeant Pepper Anderson in POLICE WOMAN. What was Pepper's first name?

13. The National Parks Service, and the men and women who make up the rangers was the background for this adventure series. What was the name of this show?

14. Curt Gowdy hosted a sports nostalgia show about athletes and sporting events. Can you name the program?

15. Who narrated a weekly documentary series about World War II titled THE WORLD AT WAR?

16. AMY PRENTISS was one of the four rotating programs that made up the NBC Sunday Mystery Movie. Who was Amy Prentiss and what actress portrayed the role?

17. _____ _____, famous for the hit recording "Ode To Billy Joe," hosted her own summer musical variety show in 1974.

18. Former LAUGH-IN personality ____ _____ became an undercover cop for the Los Angeles Police Department in the crime series ____ ____ _____ on ABC.

19. A father-daughter team, he a con artist, she wise beyond her eleven years, traveling across the midwest during the Depression years trying to make a fast dollar was the story line for this comedy. Name the program and the two stars.

20. After Sonny and his wife Cher broke up, he tried to go it alone as the host of what ABC show?

21. DEAN MARTIN'S COMEDY WORLD was a summer replacement for THE DEAN MARTIN COMEDY HOUR. Who was the host?

22. Cal McKay was an Alaskan cop nicknamed _____, from the program of the same name, starring _____ _____.

23. Five of the original cast members of GILLIGAN'S ISLAND were involved with THE NEW ADVENTURES OF GILLIGAN. How did they participate?

24. On THE NIGHT STALKER, what was the name of the reporter portrayed by Darren McGavin?

1975

1. A.M. AMERICA was the ABC network's first morning program to compete with NBC's TODAY SHOW. Who were the co-hosts?
2. On this unusual type of game show, contestants were given the opportunity to act out a scene from a motion picture with well known performers. Can you name the show?
3. Eddie Spencer and Kong were THE GHOST BUSTERS on this Saturday morning series on CBS. Who played Spencer and Kong?
4. ABC's ubiquitous sports personality, Howard Cosell, hosted a prime-time variety show which was telecast live. What was the name of the show?
5. Jeff Cable and Cash Conover were undercover agents for the governor of California in this western series. Name the series and the stars.
6. Match 1975's new game shows and their hosts.

BLANK CHECK	Adam Wade
BLANKETY BLANKS	Bob Eubanks
GIVE-N-TAKE	Bobby Van
THE MAGNIFICENT	
MARBLE MACHINE	Jim Lange
MUSICAL CHAIRS	Art James
THE NEIGHBORS	Bill Cullen

RHYME AND REASON   Dick Enberg
SHOWOFFS   Bill Carruthers
THREE FOR THE MONEY Art James

7. THE INVISIBLE MAN was a science fiction adventure series originally seen many years before with London as a setting. The 1975 adaptation took place in America and starred _____ _____ as the Invisible Man.

8. Dean Martin popularized this private eye during the 1960s in several movies. Name the character and who portrayed him on TV.

9. Hal Linden is Captain Barney Miller in the police comedy series BARNEY MILLER, but who played David, his son and Rachel, his daughter?

10. Bumper Morgan was a ____ and the lead character in the crime drama ____ ____ _____, starring ____ _____.

11. Stacy Keach starred in CARIBE. What was Caribe?

12. Dr. Jake Goodwin was the Chief of Neurosurgery at Lowell Memorial Hospital in what medical drama, and who played the role?

13. THE FAMILY HOLVAK was a very short-run drama series set in the South during the Depression. Who were the principal stars in this series?

14. After the demise of A.M. AMERICA, ABC revised its early-morning show and introduced GOOD MORNING AMERICA. Who was the original female co-host?

15. Joe Vitale and Gus Duzik were factory workers in a comedy series about a widower raising his children. Name the series and who played Joe Vitale and Gus Duzik.

16. A tough female lawyer and her father, an ex-cop, made a good team in this dramatic series. What was the name of the program and who played the tough lawyer?

17. THE ODDBALL COUPLE was a weekend morning cartoon motivated by THE ODD COUPLE. Who were the main characters?

18. Cloris Leachman starred as Phyllis Lindstrom, a

widow with a teenage daughter in the comedy series PHYLLIS. Who played the daughter?

19. S.W.A.T. was the story of a police unit organized along the same pattern as a military platoon. What does S.W.A.T. stand for?

20. Peter Campbell was a TV reporter in this hour-long adventure series. Name the series and star.

21. Dick Gautier was featured in a comedy series which lampooned the legend of Robin Hood. Name the comedy series.

22. STARSKY AND HUTCH was a successful police series about a pair of plainclothes street-wise cops who worked for a tough but understanding boss, Captain Dobey. Who played Dobey?

23. This was another "single parent raises a child" series. In this case the parent was a struggling young musician trying to raise his stepdaughter. What was the name of the show?

24. Frank McBride, an ex-cop, and Pete Ryan, an ex-con were private detectives in the hour-long series _____, starring _____ _____ and _____ _____.

1976

1. Jim Bouton starred in his own series based on his book about an inside view of baseball. What was the name of the ball club he played for in this comedy?
2. Wayne Rogers was the star of a private detective series which took place in Los Angeles during the 1930s. Name the program and the character he played.
3. Two generations of doctors, with completely different attitudes to the practice of medicine, were the lead characters in this situation comedy. What was the name of the series and who were the stars?
4. Serpico was an hour-long police drama based on the real-life experiences of a New York undercover cop, Frank Serpico. Who played him in this series?
5. Michael Constantine played a night-court judge in the comedy series _____ _____.
6. Walter Franklin, played by ___ _____, was Superior Court Judge on ___ ___ _____.
7. ALL'S FAIR was a comedy series about a forty-nine year old political columnist and his twenty-three year old photographer girlfriend. What were the names of these characters and who played them?
8. Don Rickles played Otto Sharkey in the series C.P.O.

SHARKEY. Sharkey's colleague was Chief Petty Officer Robinson. Who played Robinson?

9. Dominick Delvecchio and Paul Shonski were detective partners in the police series DELVECCHIO. Name the actors who portrayed them.

10. James Coco and Geraldine Brooks played a married couple who owned a luncheonette in a New York office building in a short-lived comedy series. Name the show.

11. "Intersect" was a government think-tank in what hour-long adventure series?

12. Robert Stack was Captain Linc Evers in the police series _____ _____.

13. A female talent agent and a Navy man married to each other provided the laughter on what comedy series?

14. What kind of a weekly series was THE QUEST?

15. SARA was a western series set in Independence, Colorado in the 1870s. What was Sara's occupation and who played her?

16. Who was the star and what kind of a weekly series was BERT D'ANGELO/SUPERSTAR?

17. Cardway Corporation was the background setting for this hour-long drama series which had an exceptionally large cast of regular characters. What was the name of the series?

18. Initially THE GONG SHOW was a daytime show for amateur talent. The winning contestant received a cash award. How much was it?

19. Mr. Angel was a messenger from the "hereafter" and granted fantasies to deserving people in the comedy series _____ _____ starring ____ _____.

20. John St. John was a real-life special investigator for the Los Angeles Police Department. This series dealt with his actual experiences and was titled _____ ____ starring _____ _____.

21. Every ethnic group at one time or another had a situation comedy series on TV. This time it was a Puerto Rican widower raising his two sons. Name the series.

22. The CBS television network began broadcasting a series of nightly BICENTENNIAL MINUTES in 1974 honoring the country's forthcoming two hundredth anniversary. What was the number of total minutes that ran in this series?
23. GONE WITH THE WIND made its television debut on the _____ network's special presentation program titled ____ ____ _____.
24. Who was the first host of the thirty-minute money game show THE $128,000 QUESTION?

1977

1. The Markowitz Family was a nice Jewish family, but it was time for their son Lenny to go off on his own in this comedy series. Name the show and who played Lenny.
2. Any time you have a slow-moving deep Southern police chief, and a black deputy who had been trained in a big-city police department you have the basic elements for a comedy series. What was the name of the show and who were the stars?
3. What kind of program was DOG AND CAT?
4. An hour-long crime drama series which featured a young female attorney and her father, an ex-conman, was titled ____ ____ ____ ____ _____, and starred _____ _____ and _____ _____.
5. What was the name of the Flint, Michigan Irish-Catholic family of six in the dramatic series of the same name?
6. _____ _____ and _____ _____ were police officers in the crime series FUTURE COP. They were responsible for training a rookie officer, who unknown to them was a _____.
7. A game show in which contestants try to predict how a celebrity would answer was titled ____ _____ _____ and hosted by ____ _____.

8. R.B. Kingston was a top investigative reporter in the newspaper drama series _____ _____, and starred _____ ____.

9. In the comedy series ____ _____ _____, principal characters Maria Teresa Bonino and Julia Peters worked for the _____ Advertising Agency.

10. Patrick McGoohan, who had played many roles as an undercover agent, finally had a change of character and became a physician in a medical drama. Name the series and the character he played.

11. Five detectives, who were children, were the leading characters in what weekend morning show?

12. A magazine format show that concentrated on people was titled WHO'S WHO. Name the three reporters associated with this program.

13. LUCAN was the story of a boy who lived with wolves until he was ten years old. Found and taught the ways of man, he adapts to society and sets out to find his natural parents. Who played the role of Lucan?

14. JAMES AT 15 and then JAMES AT 16, were the realistic stories of a teenager growing up in today's world. Who played Jamie?

15. James Hunter was a gentle soul who ran a bookstore, but in reality was a special government agent in this international adventure series. What was the name of the series and who starred as James Hunter?

16. What was the revised title for the MARY HARTMAN, MARY HARTMAN series after Louise Lasser left the show?

17. In this comedy-drama series about corporation life, all the executive positions in the company were held by women. What was the name of the series?

18. An investigative reporter for the New York Forum was the central character in this newspaper drama series. What was the name of the series and who was the star?

19. Nancy Walker played the manager of a troupe of ____ _____ _____ in the short-lived comedy series ____ _____.

20. In what series was the central character purported to

be the last survivor of the lost continent of Atlantis and who played him?

21. The Hibbards, Stuart and Judy, were a young married couple. He worked at home, she went out into the business world every day. What was the name of this comedy series?

22. A short-lived daytime serial about two families, the Cushings and Saxtons, living in a very fashionable suburb of Chicago, was the story line for this program. Can you name this soap opera?

23. Three big miniseries were presented in 1977. Can you match the networks and number of hours they were on?

ASPEN	ABC	12 hours
BLIND AMBITION	NBC	6 hours
WASHINGTON BEHIND		
CLOSED DOORS	CBS	8 hours

24. What was the name of the twenty-fourth-century science fiction series about inhabitants of the Earth not permitted to live past the age of thirty, and can you name any or all of the four leading characters?

1978

1. A daytime magazine format show featuring Bruce Jenner and Virginia Graham was hosted by ____ _____ was titled _____ _____.
2. What was the name of the political comedy series in which a senior citizen forced to retire from his job, decided to run for the U.S. Senate and won?
3. Zeb Macahan was the central character in a western drama that spanned several generations of pioneering families. Name the series and principal star.
4. An attorney who got his law degree while serving a sentence in prison was the prime character in an hour-long series. What was the name of the program and who was the star?
5. A documentary series that followed the day-to-day life of a different physician each week was titled _____.
6. Professor Charles W. Kingsfield Jr. taught contract law in the dramatic series which went off the air after one season. Name the program and the man who played Professor Kingsfield.
7. Roger Dennis was the owner of a New York escort service in a very short-lived comedy series. Name the show and its star.
8. A behind-the-scenes look at television was the story

line of a dramatic series that was cancelled after four episodes. Can you name that series?

9. Joe Namath starred as a high school coach in an ill-fated situation comedy series titled _____ _____ _____.

10. A.E.S. HUDSON STREET was a hospital comedy series which did not last too long, but do you know what A.E.S. stood for?

11. Peter Parker, alias Spiderman, was played by _____ _____ in the hour-long adventure series THE AMAZING SPIDERMAN.

12. Pricilla Barnes and Debra Clinger played reporters for a television news magazine program on what adventure drama series?

13. A thirty-minute prime-time show presented male and female celebrities competing against each other in various athletic events. Can you name the show and host?

14. Father Dan Cleary and Sister Agnes teamed up and opened a store front mission community house in a very tough neighborhood in this comedy series. What was the title of this series?

15. A romance took place in Brooklyn between an apprentice plumber and a cosmetics salesgirl in the short-run comedy series _____ _____ _____.

16. What kind of a team were the Pittsburgh Pitts?

17. A wealthy man, Jack Cole, was falsely accused and found guilty of a crime he did not commit. Upon his release from prison he tried to find the people who framed him. Name this hour-long crime show.

18. Ray Ellis deserted his wife and family for seven years and then came back to find he had been declared legally dead in this comedy series. Can you name the program?

19. Who hosted THE CHEAP SHOW?

20. In this comedy series, Harvey Kavanaugh was a long-time actor who never made it. Who played Harvey and what was the name of the program?

21. Who played Officer Dan Shay, undercover man for

the Los Angeles Police Department, in an hour-long crime drama which bears his name?

22. In THE EDDIE CAPRA MYSTERIES series, what was Eddie Capra's occupation and who played him?

23. _____ _____ was the story of three airline stewardesses who worked for Sun West Airlines.

24. Bill Cullen hosted two new game shows in 1978. What were their titles?

Photo Album

Question 1:
There goes Ted again sounding off, while Mary smirks and listens attentively for she has heard all this before. What TV station did they work for?

Question 2:
It seems Archie was always shouting at someone, either at home or at work. Can you name the company he worked for?

Question 3:
Everybody's favorite cop worked at the _____
_____ Precinct.

Question 4:
The Cunningham family and their friends continue to entertain TV audiences, but did you ever wonder what Mr. Cunningham does for a living?

Question 5:
How many years did McLean Stevenson portray Lieutenant Colonel Henry Blake, leader of the M*A*S*H group?

Question 6:
Bob Newhart seems to doubt what _____ _____ is telling him.

Question 7:
This man is a private detective who on occasion is assisted by his father. What's his dad's name?

Question 8:
Name these three actresses and the show that they are in.

Question 9:
At what school did this group spend their days?

Question 10:
Where did this housewife live?

Question 11:
What's the full name of their boss?

Question 12:
Name the two popular D.J.s at the radio station where this group works.

238

Prime-Time
Network Program
Schedules

		7PM	7:30	8PM	8:30
Sunday	ABC		Young Rebels		The F.B.I.
	CBS	Lassie	Hogan's Heroes	The Ed Sullivan Show	
	NBC	Wild Kingdom	Wonderful World of Disney		Bill Cosby Show
Monday	ABC			Young Lawyers	Silent Force
	CBS			Gunsmoke	Here's Lucy
	NBC		Red Skelton Show	Rowan & Martin's Laugh-In	
Tuesday	ABC			Mod Squad	Movie of the Week
	CBS		Beverly Hillbillies	Green Acres	Hee Haw
	NBC			Don Knotts Show	Julia
Wednesday	ABC		Courtship of Eddie's Father	Make Room For Granddaddy	Room 222
	CBS			Storefront Lawyers	Governor and J.J.
	NBC			Men From Shiloh	
Thursday	ABC			Matt Lincoln	Bewitched
	CBS		Family Affair	Jim Nabors Hour	
	NBC			Flip Wilson Show	Ironsides
Friday	ABC		Brady Bunch	Nanny and the Professor	Partridge Family
	CBS			The Interns	Head Master
	NBC			High Chaparral	Name of the Game
Saturday	ABC		Lets Make A Deal	Newlywed Game	Lawrence Welk Show
	CBS			Mission Impossible	My Three Sons
	NBC			Andy Williams Show	Adam-12

Question 1:
ROOM 222 was located at what high school?

NETWORK SCHEDULE

9PM	9:30	10PM	10:30	11PM	
		ABC Sunday Night Movie		ABC	Sunday
	Glen Campbell Goodtime Hour		Tim Conway Comedy Hour	CBS	
	Bonanza		Bold Ones	NBC	
		ABC Monday Night Football		ABC	Monday
Mayberry R.F.D.	Doris Day Show		Carol Burnett Show	CBS	
		NBC Monday Night Movie		NBC	
	Movie of the Week		Marcus Welby, M.D.	ABC	Tuesday
Hee Haw	To Rome With Love		60 Minutes/Specials	CBS	
		NBC Tuesday Night Movie		NBC	
	Johnny Cash Show		Dan August	ABC	Wednesday
	Medical Center		Hawaii Five-O	CBS	
	Kraft Music Hall		Four In One	NBC	
Barefoot in the Park	Odd Couple		The Immortal	ABC	Thursday
		CBS Thursday Night Movie		CBS	
Ironside	Nancy		Dean Martin Show	NBC	
That Girl	Love American Style		This is Tom Jones	ABC	Friday
		CBS Friday Night Movie		CBS	
	Name of the Game		Bracken's World	NBC	
Lawrence Welk Show	Most Deadly Game			ABC	Saturday
Arnie	Mary Tyler Moore Show		Mannix	CBS	
		NBC Saturday Night Movie		NBC	

	7PM	7:30	8PM	8:30
Sunday ABC				The F.B.I.
CBS			CBS Sunday Night Movie	
NBC			Wonderful World of Disney	Jimmy Stewart Show
Monday ABC			Nanny and The Professor	
CBS			Gunsmoke	
NBC			Rowan & Martin's Laugh-In	
Tuesday ABC			Mod Squad	Movie of the Week
CBS			Glen Campbell Goodtime Hour	Hawaii Five-O
NBC			Ironside	Sarge
Wednesday ABC			Bewitched	Courtship of Eddie's Father
CBS			Carol Burnett Show	
NBC			Adam-12	NBC Mystery Movie
Thursday ABC			Alias Smith & Jones	
CBS			Bearcats	
NBC			Flip Wilson Show	
Friday ABC			Brady Bunch	Partridge Family
CBS			Chicago Teddy Bears	O'Hara
NBC			The D.A.	NBC World Premiere Movie
Saturday ABC			Getting Together	ABC Movie of the Weekend
CBS			All in the Family	Funny Face
NBC			The Partners	The Good Life

Question 2:
What type of program was NICHOLS?

NETWORK
SCHEDULE

9PM	9:30	10PM	10:30	11PM	
ABC Sunday Night Movie				ABC	Sunday
CBS Sunday Night Movie		Cade's County		CBS	Sunday
Bonanza			Bold Ones	NBC	Sunday
ABC Monday Night Football				ABC	Monday
Here's Lucy	Doris Day Show	My Three Sons	Arnie	CBS	Monday
NBC Monday Night Movie				NBC	Monday
Movie of the Week			Marcus Welby M.D.	ABC	Tuesday
Hawaii Five-O		Cannon		CBS	Tuesday
Sarge		The Funny Side		NBC	Tuesday
Smith Family	Shirley's World		Man and the City	ABC	Wednesday
Medical Center			Mannix	CBS	Wednesday
NBC Mystery Movie			Night Gallery	NBC	Wednesday
Longstreet			Owen Marshall	ABC	Thursday
CBS Thursday Night Movie				CBS	Thursday
Nichols			Dean Martin Show	NBC	Thursday
Room 222	Odd Couple		Love American Style	ABC	Friday
U.S. Treasury		New CBS Friday Night Movies		CBS	Friday
NBC World Premiere Movie				NBC	Friday
ABC Movie of the Weekend			The Persuaders	ABC	Saturday
New Dick Van Dyke Show	Mary Tyler Moore Show		Mission Impossible	CBS	Saturday
NBC Saturday Night Movie				NBC	Saturday

		7PM	7:30	8PM	8:30
Sunday	ABC				The F.B.I.
	CBS		Anna and the King	M*A*S*H	Sandy Duncan Show
	NBC		Wonderful World of Disney		NBC Sunday Mystery Movie
Monday	ABC				The Rookies
	CBS				Gunsmoke
	NBC				Rowan & Martin's Laugh-In
Tuesday	ABC			Temperatures Rising	Tuesday Movie of the Week
	CBS			Maude	Hawaii Five-O
	NBC				Bonanza
Wednesday	ABC			Paul Lynde Show	Wednesday Movie of the Week
	CBS				Carol Burnett Show
	NBC			Adam-12	NBC Wednesday Mystery Movie
Thursday	ABC				Mod Squad
	CBS				The Waltons
	NBC				Flip Wilson Show
Friday	ABC			Brady Bunch	Partridge Family
	CBS				Sonny and Cher Comedy Hour
	NBC			Sanford & Son	Little People
Saturday	ABC				Alias Smith & Jones
	CBS			All in the Family	Bridget Loves Bernie
	NBC				Emergency

Question 3:
Rich Little was a regular on what show this season?

NETWORK
SCHEDULE

9PM	9:30	10PM	10:30	11PM	
ABC Sunday Night Movie				ABC	Sunday
New Dick Van Dyke Show		Mannix		CBS	
NBC Sunday Mystery Movie		Night Gallery		NBC	
ABC Monday Night Football				ABC	Monday
Here's Lucy	Doris Day Show		New Bill Cosby Show	CBS	
NBC Monday Night Movie				NBC	
Tuesday Movie of the Week		Marcus Welby M.D.		ABC	Tuesday
Hawaii Five-O		New Tuesday Night Movies		CBS	
Bold Ones		NBC Reports		NBC	
Wednesday Movie of the Week		Julie Andrews Hour		ABC	Wednesday
Medical Center		Cannon		CBS	
NBC Wednesday Mystery Movie		Search		NBC	
The Men		Owen Marshall		ABC	Thursday
CBS Thursday Night Movie				CBS	
Ironside		Dean Martin Show		NBC	
Room 222	Odd Couple	Love American Style		ABC	Friday
CBS Friday Night Movie				CBS	
Ghost Story		Banyon		NBC	
Streets of San Francisco		The Sixth Sense		ABC	Saturday
Mary Tyler Moore Show	Bob Newhart Show	Mission Impossible		CBS	
NBC Saturday Night Movie				NBC	

		7PM	7:30	8PM	8:30
Sunday	ABC			The F.B.I.	ABC Sunday Night Movie
	CBS		The New Adventures of Perry Mason		Mannix
	NBC		Wonderful World of Disney		NBC Sunday Mystery Movie
Monday	ABC			The Rookies	
	CBS			Gunsmoke	
	NBC			Lotsa Luck	Diana
Tuesday	ABC			Temperatures Rising	Tuesday Movie of the Week
	CBS			Maude	Hawaii Five-O
	NBC			Chase	
Wednesday	ABC			Bob & Carol & Ted & Alice	Wednesday Movie of the Week
	CBS			Sonny & Cher Comedy Hour	
	NBC			Adam-12	NBC Wednesday Mystery Movie
Thursday	ABC			Toma	
	CBS			The Waltons	
	NBC			Flip Wilson Show	
Friday	ABC			Brady Bunch	Odd Couple
	CBS			Calucci's Dept.	Roll Out
	NBC			Sanford & Son	The Girl With Something Extra
Saturday	ABC			Partridge Family	ABC Suspense Movie
	CBS			All in the Family	M*A*S*H
	NBC			Emergency	

Question 4:
Name the two entertainers who usually appeared on the NBC FOLLIES.

246

NETWORK
SCHEDULE

9PM	9:30	10PM	10:30	11PM	
ABC Sunday Night Movie				ABC	Sunday
Mannix		Barnaby Jones		CBS	
NBC Sunday Mystery Movie				NBC	
ABC Monday Night Football				ABC	Monday
Here's Lucy	New Dick Van Dyke Show		Medical Center	CBS	
NBC Monday Night Movie				NBC	
Tuesday Movie of the Week			Marcus Welby M.D.	ABC	Tuesday
Hawaii Five-O		Tuesday Night CBS Movie		CBS	
The Magician			Police Story	NBC	
Wednesday Movie of the Week			Owen Marshall	ABC	Wednesday
Cannon			Kojak	CBS	
NBC Wednesday Mystery Movie			Love Story	NBC	
Kung Fu			Streets of San Francisco	ABC	Thursday
CBS Thursday Night Movie				CBS	
Ironside			NBC Follies	NBC	
Room 222	Adam's Rib		Love American Style	ABC	Friday
CBS Friday Night Movie				CBS	
Needles and Pins	Brian Keith Show		Dean Martin Show	NBC	
ABC Suspense Movie			Griff	ABC	Saturday
Mary Tyler Moore Show	Bob Newhart Show		Carol Burnett Show	CBS	
NBC Saturday Night Movie				NBC	

		7PM	7:30	8PM	8:30
Sunday	ABC			Sonny Comedy Revue	
	CBS		Apple's Way		Kojak
	NBC		Wonderful World of Disney		NBC Sunday Mystery Movie
Monday	ABC			The Rookies	
	CBS			Gunsmoke	
	NBC			Born Free	
Tuesday	ABC			Happy Days	Tuesday Movie of the Week
	CBS			Good Times	M*A*S*H
	N3C			Adam-12	NBC World Premiere Movie
Wednesday	ABC			That's My Mama	Wednesday Movie of the Week
	CBS			Sons & Daughters	
	NBC			Little House on the Prairie	
Thursday	ABC			Odd Couple	Paper Moon
	CBS			The Waltons	
	NBC			Sierra	
Friday	ABC			Kodiak	Six Million Dollar Man
	CBS			Planet of the Apes	
	NBC			Sanford & Son	Chico and the Man
Saturday	ABC			The New Land	
	CBS			All in the Family	Friends and Lovers
	NBC			Emergency	

Question 5:
THAT'S MY MAMA took place in what city?

NETWORK
SCHEDULE

9PM	9:30	10PM	10:30	11PM	
		ABC Sunday Night Movie		ABC	Sunday
Kojak		Mannix		CBS	
	NBC Sunday Mystery Movie			NBC	
		ABC Monday Night Football		ABC	Monday
Maude	Rhoda		Medical Center	CBS	
	NBC Monday Night Movie			NBC	
Tuesday Movie of the Week			Marcus Welby M.D.	ABC	Tuesday
	Hawaii Five-O		Barnaby Jones	CBS	
NBC World Premiere Movie			Police Story	NBC	
Wednesday Movie of the Week			Get Christie Love	ABC	Wednesday
	Cannon		Man Hunter	CBS	
	Lucas Tanner		Petrocelli	NBC	
	Streets of San Francisco		Harry-O	ABC	Thursday
	CBS Thursday Night Movie			CBS	
	Ironside		Movin' On	NBC	
Six Million Dollar Man	Texas Wheelers		The Night Stalker	ABC	Friday
	CBS Friday Night Movie			CBS	
	Rockford Files		Police Woman	NBC	
	Kung Fu		Nakia	ABC	Saturday
Mary Tyler Moore Show	Bob Newhart Show		Carol Burnett Show	CBS	
	NBC Saturday Night Movie			NBC	

		7PM	7:30	8PM	8:30
Sunday	ABC		Swiss Family Robinson		Six Million Dollar Man
	CBS		Three For The Road		Cher
	NBC		Wonderful World of Disney		Family Holvak
Monday	ABC				Barbary Coast
	CBS			Rhoda	Phyllis
	NBC				Invisible Man
Tuesday	ABC			Happy Days	Welcome Back Kotter
	CBS			Good Times	Joe and Sons
	NBC				Movin' On
Wednesday	ABC			When Things Were Rotten	That's My Mama
	CBS				Tony Orlando and Dawn
	NBC				Little House on the Prairie
Thursday	ABC			Barney Miller	On The Rocks
	CBS				The Waltons
	NBC			The Montefuscos	Fay
Friday	ABC				Mobile One
	CBS			Big Eddie	M*A*S*H
	NBC			Sanford and Son	Chico and the Man
Saturday	ABC				Saturday Night Live with Howard Cosell
	CBS			The Jeffersons	Doc
	NBC				Emergency

Question 6:
In the short-lived comedy series BIG EDDIE, who played Eddie?

NETWORK
SCHEDULE

9PM	9:30	10PM	10:30	11PM	
		ABC Sunday Night Movie		ABC	Sunday
	Kojak		Bronk	CBS	
		NBC Sunday Mystery Movie		NBC	
		ABC Monday Night Football		ABC	Monday
All in the Family	Maude		Medical Center	CBS	
		NBC Monday Night Movie		NBC	
	The Rookies		Marcus Welby M.D.	ABC	Tuesday
	Switch		Beacon Hill	CBS	
	Police Story		Joe Forester	NBC	
	Baretta		Starsky and Hutch	ABC	Wednesday
	Cannon		Kate McShane	CBS	
	Doctors Hospital		Petrocelli	NBC	
Streets of San Francisco			Harry-O	ABC	Thursday
		CBS Thursday Night Movie		CBS	
	Ellery Queen		Medical Story	NBC	
		ABC Friday Night Movie		ABC	Friday
	Hawaii Five-O		Barnaby Jones	CBS	
	Rockford Files		Police Woman	NBC	
	S.W.A.T.		Matt Helm	ABC	Saturday
Mary Tyler Moore Show	Bob Newhart Show		Carol Burnett Show	CBS	
		NBC Saturday Night Movie		NBC	

		7PM	7:30	8PM	8:30
Sunday	ABC		Cos		Six Million Dollar Man
	CBS		60 Minutes		Sonny and Cher Show
	NBC		Wonderful World of Disney		NBC Sunday Mystery Movie
Monday	ABC				The Captain and Tennille
	CBS			Rhoda	Phyllis
	NBC				Little House on the Prairie
Tuesday	ABC			Happy Days	Laverne and Shirley
	CBS				Tony Orlando and Dawn Rainbow Hour
	NBC				Baa Baa Black Sheep
Wednesday	ABC				Bionic Woman
	CBS			Good Times	Ball Four
	NBC			The Practice	NBC Movie of the Week
Thursday	ABC			Welcome Back Kotter	Barney Miller
	CBS				The Waltons
	NBC				Gemini Man
Friday	ABC				Donny and Marie
	CBS				Spencer & Pilots
	NBC			Sanford and Son	Chico and the Man
Saturday	ABC			Holmes & Yo Yo	Mr. T and Tina
	CBS			The Jeffersons	Doc
	NBC				Emergency

Question 7:
Norman Lear, one of television's most prolific program creators, had four series on the air this season. Name them.

NETWORK SCHEDULE

9PM	9:30	10PM	10:30	11PM	
	ABC Sunday Night Movie			ABC	Sunday
	Kojak		Delvecchio	CBS	Sunday
NBC Sunday Mystery Movie		Big Event		NBC	Sunday
	ABC Monday Night Football			ABC	Monday
Maude	All's Fair		Executive Suite	CBS	Monday
	NBC Monday Night Movie			NBC	Monday
Rich Man, Poor Man-Book II			Family	ABC	Tuesday
M*A*S*H	One Day At A Time		Switch	CBS	Tuesday
	Police Woman		Police Story	NBC	Tuesday
	Baretta		Charlie's Angels	ABC	Wednesday
All in the Family	Alice		Blue Knight	CBS	Wednesday
	NBC Movie of the Week		The Quest	NBC	Wednesday
Tony Randall Show	Nancy Walker Show		Streets of San Francisco	ABC	Thursday
	Hawaii Five-O		Barnaby Jones	CBS	Thursday
	NBC Best Sellers		Van Dyke and Company	NBC	Thursday
	ABC Friday Night Movie			ABC	Friday
	CBS Friday Night Movie			CBS	Friday
	Rockford Files		Serpico	NBC	Friday
	Starsky and Hutch		Most Wanted	ABC	Saturday
Mary Tyler Moore Show	Bob Newhart Show		Carol Burnett Show	CBS	Saturday
	NBC Saturday Night Movie			NBC	Saturday

		7PM	7:30	8PM	8:30
Sunday	ABC		The Hardy Boys/ Nancy Drew Mysteries	Six Million Dollar Man	
	CBS		60 Minutes	Rhoda	On Our Own
	NBC		Wonderful World of Disney		
Monday	ABC			San Pedro Beach Bums	
	CBS			Young Dan'l Boone	
	NBC			Little House on the Prairie	
Tuesday	ABC			Happy Days	Laverne and Shirley
	CBS			The Fitzpatricks	
	NBC			Richard Pryor Show	
Wednesday	ABC			Eight Is Enough	
	CBS			Good Times	Busting Loose
	NBC			Life and Times of Grizzly Adams	
Thursday	ABC			Welcome Back Kotter	What's Happening
	CBS			The Waltons	
	NBC			Chips	
Friday	ABC			Donny and Marie	
	CBS			New Adventures of Wonder Woman	
	NBC			Sanford Arms	Chico and the Man
Saturday	ABC			Fish	Operation Petticoat
	CBS			Bob Newhart Show	We've Got Each Other
	NBC			Bionic Woman	

Question 8:
*ROSETTI AND RYAN were _____ in this short-run
series.*

NETWORK
SCHEDULE

9PM	9:30	10PM	10:30	11PM	
ABC Sunday Night Movie				ABC	Sunday
All in the Family	Alice		Kojak	CBS	Sunday
Big Event				NBC	Sunday
Monday Night Football				ABC	Monday
Betty White Show	Maude		Rafferty	CBS	Monday
NBC Monday Night Movie				NBC	Monday
Three's Company	Soap		Family	ABC	Tuesday
M*A*S*H	One Day At A Time		Lou Grant	CBS	Tuesday
Mulligan's Stew		Police Woman		NBC	Tuesday
Charlie's Angels		Baretta		ABC	Wednesday
CBS Wednesday Night Movie				CBS	Wednesday
Oregon Trail		Big Hawaii		NBC	Wednesday
Barney Miller	Carter Country	Redd Foxx Show		ABC	Thursday
Hawaii Five-O		Barnaby Jones		CBS	Thursday
Man From Atlantis		Rosetti and Ryan		NBC	Thursday
ABC Friday Night Movie				ABC	Friday
Logan's Run		Switch		CBS	Friday
Rockford Files		Quincy, M.E.		NBC	Friday
Starsky and Hutch		Love Boat		ABC	Saturday
The Jeffersons	Tony Randall Show	Carol Burnett Show		CBS	Saturday
NBC Saturday Movie				NBC	Saturday

255

		7PM	7:30	8PM	8:30
Sunday	ABC		The Hardy Boys Mysteries		Battlestar Galactica
	CBS		60 Minutes		Mary
	NBC		Wonderful World of Disney		Big Event
Monday	ABC			Welcome Back Kotter	Operation Petticoat
	CBS			WKRP in Cincinnati	People
	NBC			Little House on the Prairie	
Tuesday	ABC			Happy Days	Laverne and Shirley
	CBS			Paper Chase	
	NBC			Granpa Goes to Washington	
Wednesday	ABC			Eight is Enough	
	CBS			The Jeffersons	In the Beginning
	NBC			Dick Clark's Live Wednesday	
Thursday	ABC			Mork & Mindy	What's Happening
	CBS			The Waltons	
	NBC			Project U.F.O.	
Friday	ABC			Donny and Marie	
	CBS			New Adventures of Wonder Woman	
	NBC			Waverly Wonders	Who's Watching The Kids
Saturday	ABC			Carter Country	Apple Pie
	CBS			Rhoda	Good Times
	NBC			Chips	

Question 9:
QUINCY rarely has time to socialize, but when he does, who is the lady in his life?

NETWORK SCHEDULE

9PM	9:30	10PM	10:30	11PM	
		ABC Sunday Night Movie		ABC	Sunday
All in the Family	Alice		Kaz	CBS	
	Big Event		Life Line	NBC	
		Monday Night Football		ABC	Monday
M*A*S*H	One Day At A Time		Lou Grant	CBS	
		NBC Monday Movie		NBC	
Three's Company	Taxi		Starsky and Hutch	ABC	Tuesday
		CBS Tuesday Movie		CBS	
		Big Event		NBC	
	Charlie's Angels		Vegas	ABC	Wednesday
		CBS Wednesday Movie		CBS	
		NBC Wednesday Movie		NBC	
Barney Miller	Soap		Family	ABC	Thursday
	Hawaii Five-O		Barnaby Jones	CBS	
	Quincy, M.E.		W.E.B.	NBC	
		ABC Friday Movie		ABC	Friday
	Incredible Hulk		Flying High	CBS	
	Rockford Files		Eddie Capra Mysteries	NBC	
	Love Boat		Fantasy Island	ABC	Saturday
	American Girls		Dallas	CBS	
	Specials		Sword of Justice	NBC	

ANSWERS

1970

1. ARNIE — Arnie Nuvo/Herschel Bernardi
2. BAREFOOT IN THE PARK
3. Geraldine Jones, Reverend Leroy, and Freddie Johnson
4. An educational program for children
5. Broderick Crawford
6. THE MOST DEADLY GAME
7. Keith Jackson, Howard Cosell, and Don Meredith
8. Kevin, Laurie, Danny, Christopher, and Tracy
9. THE SILENT FORCE
10. Tim Conway
11. THE YOUNG REBELS
12. Lee J. Cobb — THE YOUNG LAWYERS
13. HAPPY DAYS
14. Andy Griffith — HEADMASTER
15. MATT LINCOLN — Psychiatry
16. Peter B. Clifford, Chief of Detectives/J.D. Cannon
17. NANCY — Renne Jarrett

18. Nanny — Juliet Mills — NANNY AND THE PRO-FESSOR
19. Murray Greshler, the cop/Al Molinaro
20. George Hamilton — PARIS 7000
21. WHERE'S HUDDLES
22. 1) McCLOUD 2) NIGHT GALLERY 3) THE PSYCHIATRIST 4) SAN FRANCISCO INTERNATIONAL AIRPORT
23. STOREFRONT LAWYERS
24. 1) A WORLD APART 2) THE BEST OF EVERYTHING 3) SOMERSET; March 30, 1970

1971

1. THE CHICAGO TEDDY BEARS
2. Robert Conrad, Harry Morgan — THE D.A.
3. THE GOOD LIFE — Larry Hagman, Donna Mills, and David Wayne
4. Mel Tormé
5. LONGSTREET — James Franciscus — blind
6. THE MAN AND THE CITY — Anthony Quinn
7. Arthur Hill and Lee Majors
8. THE PARTNERS
9. THE PERSUADERS
10. THE PET SET
11. PRIMUS — Robert Brown
12. George Kennedy
13. SHIRLEY'S WORLD — Shirley MacLaine
14. Henry Fonda — THE SMITH FAMILY
15. LIDSVILLE
16. Richard and Karen Carpenter
17. Dick Van Dyke, Hope Lange — THE NEW DICK VAN DYKE SHOW
18. BEARCATS
19. Edgar Buchanan

20. GETTING TOGETHER — Bobby Sherman and Wes Stern
21. John Schuck/Sergeant Charles Enright
22. THE REEL GAME — Jack Barry
23. Sandy Duncan
24. Joe Garagiola

1972

1. Bernie's parents were played by Harold J. Stone and Bibi Osterwald; Bridget's parents were played by David Doyle and Audra Lindley
2. THE DON RICKLES SHOW — Don Rickles
3. Dr. Kelly Brackett/Robert Fuller
4. Kwai Chang Caine
5. Hugh O'Brian, Tony Franciosa, and Doug McClure — SEARCH
6. THE SIXTH SENSE — Gary Collins
7. Stone/Karl Malden — Steve/Michael Douglas — THE STREETS OF SAN FRANCISCO
8. Supreme Headquarters, Alien Defense Organization — UFO
9. Samantha Eggar
10. Robert Forster
11. Dogs — THE BARKLEYS
12. Jerry Robinson/Peter Bonerz
13. THE LITTLE PEOPLE — Brian Keith and Shelley Fabares
14. ME AND THE CHIMP — Ted Bessell
15. Sam Groom — POLICE SURGEON
16. THE PROTECTORS

17. Georg Stanford Brown, Michael Ontkean, and Sam Melville
18. Tom Bosley
19. SPLIT SECOND
20. Mark Jenkins played Dr. Gildare, Gary Merrill played Dr. Gillespie
21. Joe Girelli/Richard S. Castallano
22. Attorney
23. ASSIGNMENT VIENNA, DELPHI BUREAU, and JIGSAW
24. Wink Martindale

1973

1. Ken Howard and Blythe Danner
2. James Coco, State Unemployment Office — CALUCCI'S DEPARTMENT
3. THE GIRL WITH SOMETHING EXTRA — Sally Field
4. Detective — GRIFF
5. Billy Jim Hawkins — HAWKINS
6. THE MARCUS — NELSON MURDERS
7. LOTSA LUCK — Dom DeLuise
8. A) Monte Markham B) Sharon Acker C) Harry Guardino D) Dane Clark
9. Julie Harris, Richard Long — THICKER THAN WATER
10. Tony Musante
11. A TOUCH OF GRACE — Shirley Booth, J. Pat O'Malley
12. CHASE
13. Peggy Cass
14. LOVE THY NEIGHBOR
15. Loud — AN AMERICAN FAMILY
16. Diana Rigg — DIANA
17. INCH HIGH, PRIVATE EYE

18. ROLL OUT
19. DUSTY'S TRAIL
20. OZZIE'S GIRLS
21. Ernesta . . . . Helen Hayes
    Gwen . . . . Mildred Natwick
22. Bob/Robert Urich, Carol/Ann Archer, Ted/David
    Spielberg, Alice/Anita Gillette
23. DOC ELLIOT — James Franciscus
24. 1) TOMORROW — Monday through Thursday
       nights
    2) THE MIDNIGHT SPECIAL — Friday night

1974

1. Ronny Cox — APPLE'S WAY
2. Gary Collins and Diana Muldaur
3. Don Benedict and Jim McMullan
4. DIRTY SALLY
5. FIREHOUSE — James Drury
6. David Janssen — HARRY-O
7. JACKPOT
8. LUCAS TANNER — David Hartman
9. Ken Howard — THE MANHUNTER
10. Sonny Pruitt, Will Chandler
11. PETROCELLI — Barry Newman
12. Suzanne
13. SIERRA
14. THE WAY IT WAS
15. Sir Laurence Olivier
16. Chief of Detectives, San Francisco Police Department — Jessica Walter
17. Bobbie Gentry
18. Teresa Graves — GET CHRISTIE LOVE
19. PAPER MOON — Christopher Connelly and Jodie Foster
20. THE SONNY COMEDY REVUE

21. Jackie Cooper
22. Kodiak — Clint Walker
23. Through their voices, because the new series was animated.
24. Carl Kolchak

1975

1. Bill Beutel and Stephanie Edwards
2. Don Adams — SCREEN TEST
3. Larry Storch and Forrest Tucker
4. SATURDAY NIGHT LIVE WITH HOWARD COSELL
5. BARBARY COAST — William Shatner, Doug McClure
6. BLANK CHECK .... Art James
   BLANKETY BLANKS .... Bill Cullen
   GIVE-N-TAKE .... Jim Lange
   THE MAGNIFICENT MARBLE MACHINE .... Art James
   MUSICAL CHAIRS .... Adam Wade
   THE NEIGHBORS .... Bill Carruthers
   RHYME AND REASON .... Bob Eubanks
   SHOWOFFS .... Bobby Van
   THREE FOR THE MONEY ..... Dick Enberg
7. David McCallum
8. Matt Helm/Tony Franciosa
9. Michael Tessier and Anne Wyndham
10. Cop — THE BLUE KNIGHT — George Kennedy

11. A law enforcement unit working out of Miami, responsible for fighting crime in the Caribbean.
12. DOCTORS' HOSPITAL — George Peppard
13. Glenn Ford and Julie Harris
14. Nancy Dussault
15. JOE AND SONS — Richard Castellano and Jerry Stiller
16. KATE McSHANE — Anne Meara
17. Spiffy, a neat cat, and Fleabag, a messy dog
18. Lisa Gerritsen
19. Special Weapons and Tactics
20. MOBILE ONE — Jackie Cooper
21. WHEN THINGS WERE ROTTEN
22. Bernie Hamilton
23. SUNSHINE
24. SWITCH — Eddie Albert, Robert Wagner

1976

1. Washington Americans
2. CITY OF ANGELS — Jake Axminster
3. THE PRACTICE — Danny Thomas and David Spielberg
4. David Birney
5. SIROTA'S COURT
6. Tony Randall — THE TONY RANDALL SHOW
7. Richard Barrington/Richard Crenna — Charlotte (Charley) Drake — Bernadette Peters
8. Harrison Page
9. Delvecchio/Judd Hirsh — Shonski/Charles Haid
10. THE DUMPLINGS
11. GEMINI MAN
12. MOST WANTED
13. THE NANCY WALKER SHOW
14. Western
15. School teacher, Brenda Vaccaro
16. Paul Sorvino — police show
17. EXECUTIVE SUITE
18. $512.32
19. GOOD HEAVENS — Carl Reiner
20. JIGSAW JOHN — Jack Warden

21. POPI
22. 912 (July 4, 1974-December 31, 1976)
23. NBC — THE BIG EVENT
24. Mike Darrow

1977

1. BUSTING LOOSE — Adam Arkin
2. CARTER COUNTRY — Victor French/police chief
   — Kene Holiday/deputy
3. Police drama
4. THE FEATHER AND FATHER GANG — Stefanie
   Powers and Harold Gould
5. THE FITZPATRICKS
6. Ernest Borgnine — John Amos — robot
7. THE HOLLYWOOD CONNECTION — Jim Lange
8. KINGSTON: CONFIDENTIAL — Raymond Burr
9. ON YOUR OWN — Bedford
10. RAFFERTY — Dr. Sidney Rafferty
11. THE RED HAND GANG
12. Dan Rather, Barbara Howar, and Charles Kuralt
13. Kevin Brophy
14. Lance Kerwin
15. HUNTER — James Franciscus
16. FOREVER FERNWOOD
17. ALL THAT GLITTERS
18. THE ANDROS TARGETS — James Sutorius
19. Las Vegas showgirls — BLANSKY'S BEAUTIES
20. THE MAN FROM ATLANTIS — Patrick Duffy

21. WE'VE GOT EACH OTHER
22. LOVERS AND FRIENDS
23. ASPEN . . . . NBC . . . . 6 hours
    BLIND AMBITION . . . . CBS . . . . 8 hours
    WASHINGTON BEHIND
    CLOSED DOORS . . . . ABC . . . . . . 12 hours
24. LOGAN'S RUN — Logan, Jessica, Rem, and Francis

1978

1. Jack Linkletter — AMERICA ALIVE
2. GRANDPA GOES TO WASHINGTON
3. HOW THE WEST WAS WON — James Arness
4. KAZ — Ron Leibman
5. LIFELINE
6. THE PAPER CHASE — John Houseman
7. THE TED KNIGHT SHOW — Ted Knight
8. W.E.B.
9. THE WHAVERLY WONDERS
10. Adult Emergency Squad
11. Nicholas Hammond
12. THE AMERICAN GIRLS
13. CELEBRITY CHALLENGE OF THE SEXES — Tom Brookshier
14. IN THE BEGINNING
15. JOE AND VALERIE
16. A women's roller derby team
17. SWORD OF JUSTICE
18. BABY, I'M BACK
19. Dick Martin
20. Harvey Korman — THE HARVEY KORMAN SHOW

21. David Cassidy — DAVID CASSIDY — MAN UNDERCOVER
22. He was an attorney — Vincent Baggetta
23. FLYING HIGH
24. PASS THE BUCK and THE LOVE EXPERTS

THE 1970's PHOTO AND PROGRAM SCHEDULE ANSWERS

Photo Answers

1. WJM-TV, Channel 12
2. Prendergast Tool And Die Company
3. Manhattan South
4. He manages a hardware store
5. Three years
6. Marcia Wallace
7. Joseph "Rocky" Rockford
8. Top: Mackenzie Phillips, Valerie Bertinelli
   Bottom: Bonnie Franklin
9. At James Buchanan High School
10. Fernwood, Ohio
11. Charlie Townsend
12. Dr. Johnny Fever (the morning man) and Venus Flytrap (the night man)

Program Schedule Answers

1. Walt Whitman
2. Western
3. THE JULIE ANDREWS HOUR
4. Sammy Davis Jr. and Mickey Rooney
5. Washington, D.C.
6. Sheldon Leonard
7. MAUDE, ALL'S FAIR, THE JEFFERSONS, ALL IN THE FAMILY
8. Lawyers
9. Lee Potter

About The Author

Fred Goldstein is a native New Yorker and a TV buff. His interest in television has enabled him to acquire a vast knowledge of the medium's programs and stars. He has enthusiasm in many diverse areas and he develops book ideas on a wide variety of subject matters.